Turning *the* *Secret* Pages of our EXISTENCE

Unveiling the Hidden Melodies of Life

Siddharth Goswami

BookLeaf Publishing

India | USA | UK

Acknowledgement

Writing this book has been a personal discovery, exploration, and learning journey. I want to thank all the people with me, who helped and encouraged me during the creation of this work. Particularly, I would like to express my gratitude to the editor of this book, whose suggestions and comments played an important role in its creation. Your dedication to refining my work has consistently been evident. Thanks to the Almighty, whose grace and power helped me write this book. His light turned these pages. I am grateful to all my mentors and teachers in school and college for teaching me English, which has been crucial throughout my path. Thank you to Miss Raina Singh, my Professional Communication lecturer, for motivating me to write poetry in college. Her encouragement and support have aided my growth, and I am grateful. I also thank Mr. Ravinder Bhatnagar for his persistent efforts to assist me master English grammar and Conceptual comprehension. Finally, I want to sincerely thank every reader who started this book. May this book inspire you to open your heart, discover the secrets of life, and embrace its mysteries.

With gratitude,

Siddharth Goswami

About the Author

Siddharth Goswami is a B.Tech. Biotechnology graduate from Graphic Era Deemed to be University, Dehradun, India, in 2023. Siddharth is a researcher, writer, poet, and philanthropist. His several IEEE,  Scopus, and Web of Science research publications and abstracts earned him the Bank of Baroda Achievers Award. Despite his academic brilliance, Siddharth enjoys writing poetry. The Indian Prime Minister's Office praised his poem "Corona: Darkar Nahi, Ladkar" for its influential lyrics. "Turning the Secret Pages of Our Existence" expresses Siddharth's desire to write better. He wants readers to go into the pages and see the world through his eyes.

Preface

Peripheral objects and concerns, along with sensational and visible realities, easily overshadow ideas in a society filled with noise and clamor. However, another world lies just beneath the veil of daily routine and apparent reality, full of mysteries, covert influences, and unspoken realities that define us and our choices. This work, translated as *Turning the Secret Pages of Our Existence*, urges us to embrace the unknown and explore hidden quarters, times, spaces, and more that remain hidden from our view.

This book is an exploration of the darkness of our existence—the unremarked hours, forgotten aspirations, secret decisions, and covert actions. It is a depiction of the unknown origins of our lives, the murmurs of unheard ideas that may loom in our heads, and the resonance of abandoned locations and timeliness that may still echo within us today.

Every chapter is conceived as a separate story telling readers about the aspects of life that are often kept secret—from the things hidden in the heart of the silent nature to the beauty that lies in the cracks and flaws. Overall, these narratives constitute generations' histories and reflect people's efforts to understand the world and their place in it.

Turning the Secret Pages of Our Existence is more than just a story about revealing secrets; it is also about surrendering to the mysteries and finding meaning in them. It is about understanding the probabilistic structures of destiny and the music that nobody hears, but all of us dance to. It is about masculinity and the ability to persevere in times of hardship, even when one feels broken.

As you flip through these pages, I implore you to ponder the journey that you have had. Think about how the hands of time moulded you, the mystery of the strength that kept you going, and the voices of the darkness that led you through the doors to the unknown. This book may challenge each of you to break the pattern, to break the mould, and to seek the answers to your enigma. We are all enigmas. It's the light hidden within the darkness of ordinary life's shadows. I would like to thank you for being with me throughout this process. Perhaps the secrets in these pages will

help you cross the chasm into your ineffable
essence.

With gratitude,

Siddharth Goswami

Contents

Chapter 1. The Unseen Beginnings

In the quiet stir of dawn's first light,
I, Siddharth Goswami, pondered the flight
Of time and space, the cosmic dance,
That stirred existence from its primal trance.

In the cradle of void, where silence grew,
I sensed the birth of all that's new.
The whispers of creation, soft and deep,
Awoke the secrets that the cosmos keep.

From the darkened womb of endless night,
Where stars were born from purest light,
I traced the lines of hidden lore,
That spoke of what had been before.

In the abyss where dreams and matter meet,
Where echoes of the past and future greet,
I wandered paths both old and rare,
To seek the threads that weave the air.

The universe, a silent book of lore,
Revealed its pages I had not seen before.
Through veils of dust and cosmic mist,
The genesis of life, so softly kissed.

I saw the birth of rivers, valleys wide,
Where ancient secrets in shadows hide.
The unseen forces, fierce and grand,
Played their role in shaping land.

In every whisper of the wind,
In every star's celestial spin,
The hidden patterns danced in grace,
As time's first footsteps left their trace.

With each dawn, the world unfurled,
From the womb of darkness, a new world.
I beheld the silence, deep and vast,
Where the echoes of creation passed.

In the deep, uncharted sea of space,
Where primal forces leave no trace,
I found the whispers of the dawn,
That heralded the birth of life, reborn.

With every beat of cosmic heart,
From the fabric where the stars depart,
I felt the pulse of beginnings unseen,
In every shadow and every beam.

In the cradle of the silent void,
Where the primal forces once employed,
I traced the origins, soft and pure,
In the tapestry of life's allure.

The secrets of the start, so deep,
In the quiet realms where shadows sleep,
Spoke to me of mysteries grand,
Of the hidden hands that shape the land.

From the silence of the void, a spark,
A genesis of light in the dark,
I saw the universe begin its song,
A melody that would forever belong.

In the birth of stars, the rise of light,
In the dance of day and endless night,
I saw the hidden forces play,
In the canvas of the cosmic fray.

Each element, a silent prayer,
In the sacred space where none compare,
Spoke to me of beginnings old,
In stories of creation, quietly told.

As I, Siddharth Goswami, penned these lines,
In the silent realm where destiny aligns,
I uncovered truths from realms unseen,
In the poetry of the cosmic sheen.

The unseen beginnings, profound and true,
Revealed in every shadow and every hue,
Speak of mysteries that forever remain,
In the quiet whisper of creation's refrain.

And so I wander through the cosmic sea,
In the quest for truths that are meant to be,
Turning the pages of existence, I find,
The hidden forces that shape the mind.

In the echoes of beginnings, deep and vast,
I trace the steps of the cosmic past,
And in these lines, the secrets lie,
Of the unseen beginnings that touch the sky.

In the endless dance of creation's might,
I, Siddharth Goswami, in the silent night,
Find the hidden truths that gently sing,
Of the unseen beginnings, eternal spring.

Chapter 2. Whispers of the Unspoken

In the stillness where shadows play,
I, Siddharth Goswami, find my way,
Through echoes of a silent realm,
Where words are lost, yet thoughts
overwhelm.

In the quiet depths where secrets lie,
The unspoken whispers never die.
They weave through the silence, soft and
clear,
A language of the heart, if you'll hear.

In the hidden corners of the mind,
Where thoughts are left unrefined,
I hear the whispers, faint but strong,
Of truths that in silence belong.

I wander through the silent night,
Where unspoken truths take flight.
In the hush of the moon's soft glow,
The depth of silence starts to show.

From the first breath of the morning dew,
To the silence of the evening blue,
I feel the echoes of the unsaid,
In the spaces where words have fled.

The unspoken thoughts, so pure, so deep,
In the quiet moments, they silently creep.
They form the tapestry of the unseen,
In the silent echoes, soft and serene.

In the rustling leaves, in the gentle breeze,
I sense the silence with such ease.
It speaks in tones of a muted song,
Of where the unspoken thoughts belong.

Each pause in conversation's stream,
Holds the weight of a hidden dream.
The silence speaks with a voice so wise,
In the spaces where true meaning lies.

In the dance of shadows, the silence spins,
Where the unspoken truth begins.
I trace the path of the quiet's grace,
In the folds of time and space.

With every heartbeat and every sigh,
The unspoken whispers softly fly.
In the stillness of the night's embrace,
I find the truth in the silent space.

In the gaze that lingers, the touch that's brief,
In the silence that follows, I find relief.
The unspoken words, the hidden glint,
In the quiet moments, the truth is hint.

From the silent dawn to the twilight's fall,
The whispers of the unspoken call.
I listen to the silence, so profound,
In the echoes where the truth is found.

Through the veil of the unspoken,
The truth of existence is softly spoken.
I, Siddharth Goswami, hear the call,
In the silent whispers, I find it all.

In the spaces between each breath,
In the quiet that follows death,
The unspoken speaks with a voice so clear,
Of the truths that in silence appear.

With every word left unspoken,
With every silence gently broken,
I discover the depths of the unseen,
In the whispers of what might have been.

In the quiet reflection of the soul,
The unspoken whispers make me whole.
They weave a tapestry of silent grace,
In the quiet moments, I find my place.

In the hushed tones of the evening's calm,
The unspoken thoughts are like a balm.
They heal the wounds that words cannot
mend,
In the silent whispers, I find a friend.

So here I stand in the silent space,
With the unspoken truths I embrace.
In the quiet realms where whispers play,
I, Siddharth Goswami, find my way.

In the echoes of the silent night,
The unspoken truths come into sight.
With every whisper, soft and clear,
The secrets of existence, I hold dear.

Through the whispers of the unspoken,
In the silence, I am awoken.
I, Siddharth Goswami, in the quiet see,
The profound truths that set me free.

Chapter 3. Veils of Forgotten Dreams

In the quiet spaces of the heart's deep room,
I, Siddharth Goswami, chase the echoes of
lost bloom.
Dreams once bright, now shrouded in time,
Veiled in the mists of forgotten rhyme.

Have you ever wondered, as daylight fades,
What happens to dreams in life's charades?
Do they vanish like mist in the morning sun,
Or do they linger, waiting for their turn?

I look back to the days when hopes soared
high,
When stars seemed closer in the evening sky.
What happened to those dreams, so fierce and
new?
Did they disappear, or are they hiding from
view?

In life's long maze, where paths entwine,
Do old dreams still softly shine?
Are they lost in the rush of day,
Or hidden, waiting to show the way?

Those dreams we shelved, the aims we missed,
Do they linger, wrapped in mist?
Do they murmur in the quiet night,
Or fade away, out of sight?

Think of the dreams that slipped from view,
Once bright passions, now askew.
Do they whisper, though faint and rare,
Or lie dormant, wrapped in despair?

When your mind drifts in calm reprieve,
Do old dreams visit as you believe?
Do they speak of roads untraveled far,
Of hopes dimmed but not marred?

In the stillness where shadows play,
Do dreams return, lighting the way?
Are they echoes from a distant place,
Or waiting still, with a gentle grace?

Recall the dreams of youthful fire,
The ones that spoke of pure desire.
Are they now veiled by life's demand,
Or do they stir, despite the sand?

In the vaults of time, where thoughts reside,
Are old dreams still your silent guide?
Do they hold wisdom yet to share,
Or have they vanished in despair?

What if these dreams were seeds of gold,
Waiting for you to be bold?
What if they could bloom with a spark,
Turning shadows into light's mark?

Can you recall the dreams that once glowed
bright,
That filled your heart with pure delight?
Are they still woven in your soul's song,
Or have they faded, where they don't belong?

In the deep recesses of your mind,
Are there dreams you've left behind?
Are they shadows in the corridors of thought,
Or are they waiting, still unsought?

In my journey, I ponder these silent calls,
The dreams that linger, behind life's walls.
I seek the truth in their whispered plea,
To uncover what these veils might be.

So, dear reader, what of your dreams now?
Are they like old books gathering dust,
somehow?

Or do they still shimmer, though unseen,
In the depths of your soul's evergreen?

Have you ever felt that old dream's embrace,
In a moment of stillness, a quiet place?
Does it stir a memory, a silent cheer,
Of a hope that once seemed so near?

In this chapter, we unveil the dreams of old,
Those forgotten hopes that once were bold.
We explore their whispers, their silent cries,
In the veils of forgotten dreams, where truth
lies.

Siddharth Goswami, in these lines you find,
The search for dreams left behind.
Do these dreams still hold a part of you,
Or have they vanished, like morning dew?

Let us ponder these veils, so soft and thin,
The dreams we've set aside, where do they
begin?
In the quiet moments, in the silent streams,
We find the truth in forgotten dreams.

Chapter 4. Secrets Beneath the Surface

In the quiet depths where shadows fall,
I, Siddharth Goswami, heed the call,
To unveil truths beneath the guise,
Where hidden secrets softly lie.

Each morning comes with a soft embrace,
Yet hidden 'neath its golden grace,
Are echoes from the night's embrace,
Mysteries deep I yearn to trace.

The day, it shines with simple gleams,
But underneath, there's more it seems,
A dance of shadows, light and dreams,
Where thoughts flow free in silent streams.

The smile I show, a practiced art,
Yet underneath, it shields my heart,
Laughter masks the quiet cries,
Joy hides the tears in tired eyes.

In every word and fleeting glance,
A story waits, a secret dance,
A tale of fears, of love, of pain,
Of hopes unspoken, tears like rain.

I dive beneath the calmest sea,
Where truth lies lost in memory,
In whispers soft, in currents strong,
I find the echoes of my song.

The surface speaks of calm and peace,
Yet underneath, the shadows lease,
A depth where hidden passions rise,
Where unseen realms of dreams abide.

Through every touch and fleeting glance,
In every silence, there's a dance,
Of hidden truths and veiled intent,
In daily lives, their essence spent.

The pages turn with every breath,
Unfolding tales of life and death,
In secret places, deep and vast,
Where memories and dreams are cast.

What lies beneath the surface bright,
Is where the soul finds pure delight,
In simple moments, deep and true,
The essence of existence, view.

I, Siddharth, seek the depths unknown,
In every touch, in every tone,
For in the quiet, subtle sway,
The secrets of existence lay.

The mundane veil, a fleeting art,
Conceals the beating of the heart,
Yet in the spaces, deep and still,
The soul's true voice, a gentle thrill.

So as I turn these secret pages,
Through life's unspoken, ancient sages,
I find beneath the daily light,
A world that dances out of sight.

In the echoes of the hidden song,
In the quiet where the spirits throng,
I find the secrets, soft and pure,
Beneath the surface, I endure.

Through every breath and every sigh,
In simple truths that softly lie,
I, Siddharth Goswami, seek and find,
The depth of life, in heart and mind.

So let me turn these pages bright,
To explore the depths beneath the light,
For in the secrets, dark and clear,
I find the essence of what's near.

In every shadow, every grace,
The secrets of our human race,
I, Siddharth, cherish and behold,
The hidden stories softly told.

Through each unspoken, fleeting glance,
In every moment's quiet dance,
I seek the truths that lie beneath,
In the layers where secrets breathe.

And as I journey through this tome,
In hidden realms, I find my home,
For in the depths, both dark and wide,
The secrets of existence hide.

Chapter 5. Echoes of the Hidden Past

I am Siddharth Goswami, seeking light,
In shadows of the past where echoes fight,
Through corridors of time, I wander free,
In search of whispers that define me.

The past, a cloak both heavy and profound,
Its echoes shape the present all around,
In every shadow, every silent glance,
Lie the secrets of the past, a ghostly dance.

Have you ever wondered, dear soul,
How past missteps shape the present whole?
In the quiet moments, do you hear,
The echoes of what once was near?

Through hidden halls where memories sleep,
Where secrets in the dark do gently weep,
I trace the patterns of my faded past,
In hopes that understanding will last.

In childhood dreams and youthful fears,
In every joy and hidden tears,
The echoes of what once was true,
Shape the path I now pursue.

Do you recall a moment lost in time,
When choices made felt so sublime?
Yet now, in the mirror of today,
Do those echoes quietly sway?

For every wound and every scar,
The past has left a lingering mark afar,
In every heartbeat, every breath of mine,
The hidden past intertwines.

I seek to understand what lies beneath,
The whispered secrets and the silent sheath,
For in the shadows, deep and dense,
Lie truths that shape my present tense.

What of the dreams we used to chase?
Are they hidden in the past's embrace?
Do they echo in our daily plight,
Guiding us through the darkest night?

In moments of quiet, do you find,
The whispers of the past intertwined?
Do you listen to the echoes soft and clear,
Or silence them, too afraid to hear?

The past is not just a distant shore,
But a presence felt evermore,
In the choices made, in paths we tread,
The echoes of the past are often led.

Do you see how past and present blend,
In ways that seldom seem to end?
In every story, every twist and turn,
The echoes of the past eternally burn.

As I walk through this labyrinth of time,
I seek the echoes, both dark and sublime,
To understand the silent, hidden song,
That guides me as I journey along.

In every shadow, every fleeting thought,
In every lesson that the past has taught,
I find the echoes of what once was near,
Guiding my steps with a voice sincere.

So let us delve into the past so deep,
Where hidden echoes softly seep,
For in the whispers, both faint and loud,
Lie the truths that make us proud.

Do you hear the echoes of your own tale?
In every memory, in every detail?
Are you ready to confront what's been,
And let the past shape what lies within?

For Siddharth, the echoes of the past,
Are not just shadows, but a guide steadfast,
In every whisper, every hidden trace,
I find the essence of my human race.

Let us embrace the past with grace and might,
And let its echoes guide us to the light,
For in the hidden depths of what once was,
We find the echoes that define who we
become.

Chapter 6. The Enigma of Choices

I am Siddharth Goswami, pondering deep,
On choices made, and paths we keep.
The enigma of decisions, vast and wide,
Shapes our journey, far and wide.

In every moment, a choice unfolds,
A mystery in stories untold.
Do you feel the weight of each decision?
Does it steer your path with precision?

Choices, they say, are like shadows cast,
Reflecting futures, both present and past.
In the quiet of dawn, or the dead of night,
How do you choose what feels right?

I trace my steps through time's embrace,
In every choice, a hidden trace.
Do you see how choices intertwine,
Creating a life, both yours and mine?

What guides us when we stand at the fork,
In paths divergent, where do we embark?
Is it fear, hope, or fate's decree,
That shapes the choices we let be?

Each decision, a ripple in the stream,
Altering destinies, or so it seems.
Do you wonder if the choice was true,
Or if another path might have been due?

From dawn's first light to twilight's end,
Our choices mold, they shape, they blend.
How much of our fate is ours to steer,
And how much is driven by the fear?

The enigma of choices, a puzzle grand,
In every decision, where do we stand?
Is it the heart or the mind that guides,
In the quiet moments when truth hides?

I ponder on the crossroads faced,
On dreams pursued and lives erased.
Do you feel the weight of choices made,
In every dawn and every shade?

For every choice, a consequence unfurls,
In the tapestry of our swirling worlds.
What are the hidden forces at play,
In the choices made each passing day?

In every choice, a lesson lies,
A truth to find beneath the guise.
Do you seek the meaning behind each choice,
Or let the echoes fade without a voice?

The enigma of choices, ever so vast,
In every decision, echoes of the past.
Do you see the patterns, the threads unseen,
In the tapestry of your life's grand scheme?

For Siddharth, the choices weave,
A complex pattern, hard to perceive.
In every choice, a story's told,
In every path, new and old.

Do you ponder on the choices made,
In every decision, the shadows played?
Are you aware of the forces that guide,
In the silent whispers where secrets reside?

As I journey through the maze of time,
I seek the answers, profound and prime.
In every choice, I find a clue,
To the enigma of what's old and new.

So let us embrace the choices made,
In every decision, the past's cascade.
For in the enigma, we find our way,
In the choices we make each day.

Do you understand the weight you bear,
In every choice, both bold and rare?
For Siddharth, the enigma unfolds,
In the choices made, the story's told.

Chapter 7. Shadows of the Unfamiliar

In the twilight of our daily stride,
Lies a realm where shadows hide.
Beyond the comfort of the known,
Lurks the unfamiliar, dark and alone.

Have you felt the chill of the unknown,
The eerie silence where seeds are sown?
In the depths of your soul, do fears arise,
At the mere whisper of unseen skies?

The shadows dance on the edge of light,
Mysterious figures in the dead of night.
What lies beyond this veil so thin?
A question deep, where do I begin?

Do you wander through the fog of doubt,
Seeking answers that drift about?
In the face of uncertainty, where do you
stand,
When the unfamiliar takes your hand?

The unknown is a shadowy sea,
A vast expanse where we long to be.
Yet fear often grips the heart so tight,
When faced with the darkness of night.

How do you confront the fears inside,
The echoes of doubts you cannot hide?
Is it courage or is it despair,
That guides you through the shadows' lair?

In the labyrinth of the unseen and strange,
We wander through a world of change.
What drives us to explore the deep,
When the unknown makes our spirits weep?

The shadows of the unfamiliar play,
In every moment, in every day.
Do you see them dance in the periphery,
Or do you confront them with clarity?

The unknown often seems so vast,
A chasm that shadows have cast.
How do you navigate the uncharted land,

When the terrain is hard to understand?

In every shadow, a story lies,
A mystery hidden from our eyes.
What secrets do these shadows hold,
In the depths of the dark and cold?

Do you fear the darkness, or embrace its call,
When the shadows of the unfamiliar fall?
What drives you to seek beyond the night,
To unravel the mysteries just out of sight?

In the quiet of the unknown's embrace,
We seek answers in an empty space.
Do you trust the journey through the dark,
Or do you hesitate at the unknown's mark?

The unfamiliar shadows serve as a guide,
For the parts of ourselves we often hide.
What revelations await in the dark,
When we venture beyond the familiar's spark?

How do you deal with the fears that loom,
In the silence of the unknown's room?
Is it hope or dread that fuels your quest,
To uncover what lies beyond the rest?

The shadows of the unfamiliar ask,
For courage to lift the hidden mask.

Do you find the strength to see the truth,
Or does fear keep you from the unknown's
proof?

In the dance of shadows, a chance to grow,
To face the unknown and let it show.
What will you discover when you dare,
To embrace the shadows lurking there?

The journey through the unfamiliar haze,
Is a path of discovery and wonder's gaze.
Do you walk this path with a heart so bold,
Or do the shadows leave you cold?

In the end, the shadows teach us well,
In the dark, there's much to tell.
Do you see the light in the unfamiliar night,
Or does the darkness cloud your sight?

Embrace the shadows, let them guide,
Through the realm where fears reside.
For in the heart of the unknown's land,
We find the strength to understand.

So when you face the shadows near,
Let courage replace the fear.
For the unfamiliar holds a key,
To the depths of who we're meant to be.

Chapter 8. The Secret of Connections

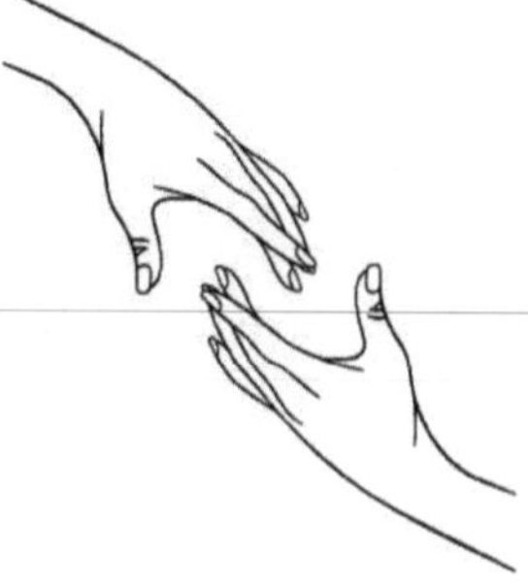

In the quiet spaces between our breaths,
Where the heart finds solace, not just regrets,
Lie secrets of connections, deep and unseen,
Threads that bind us in places we've never
been.

Have you felt the invisible threads that tie,
Your soul to others, beneath the vast sky?
In moments of silence, do you sense their
pull,
The connections unspoken, gentle yet full?

In the midst of chaos, where do we find
The delicate links that shape and bind?
Is it in a glance, a touch, a word,
Or in the silence when nothing is heard?

Do you notice the way paths intertwine,
As if by design, so perfectly aligned?
Are we not just wanderers in a grand design,
Bound by the stars, as the fates intertwine?

The secrets of connections weave a tale,
Of lives converging where destinies sail.
How do you perceive the bonds that grow,
In the moments of clarity, or when shadows
flow?

Have you ever marveled at the serendipity,
Of meeting someone, feeling the affinity?
Is it mere chance, or a deeper plan,
That guides our hearts and hand in hand?

When two souls meet, is it fate or choice,
That brings them together, gives them a
voice?
How do these connections shape who we are,
As we travel through life, beneath each star?

In every encounter, there lies a spark,
An echo of connections, a light in the dark.
Do you cherish the bonds that come and go,
Or do you question their purpose, their ebb
and flow?

The web of connections is intricate, vast,
Linking past to present, future to past.
What do you make of these threads that bind,
In the fabric of life, intricately designed?

Have you ever wondered why we meet,
Certain people whose paths seem so sweet?
Is there a reason behind these cosmic ties,
Or do they form by chance, beneath the skies?

Do you see the patterns in the way lives cross,
The hidden connections, the gain and the
loss?
In the tapestry of existence, where do you
stand,
As the threads of connection stretch across
the land?

When you feel a connection that seems so
right,
Is it a reflection of the hidden light?
Or a glimpse into a world we seldom see,
Where connections are more than just you
and me?

The secrets of connections often remain,
Hidden in the depths, beyond the mundane.
What do you think of the bonds that we
share,
Invisible threads woven with care?

How do these connections influence your
days,
In the quiet moments, in the myriad ways?
Do they shape your path, your joys, your
strife,
As you navigate the intricate maze of life?

In the realm of connections, what truths lie,
Beyond the surface, beneath the sky?
Do you embrace the mystery, the unknown,
Of how we're all linked, how we've grown?

The secret of connections is both vast and
small,
A network of bonds that cradle us all.
What revelations do you find in these ties,
As you explore the secrets, beneath the skies?

As you journey through life's intricate dance,
Do you see the connections, the fleeting
chance?
Or do you search for meaning in the silent
space,
Where connections whisper, leaving a trace?

The secret of connections is a story untold,
A narrative of bonds, of hearts and souls.
Do you find solace in the hidden embrace,
Of the connections that shape the human
race?

Chapter 9. Veiled Moments of Clarity

In the labyrinth of life, where shadows play,
I find myself seeking the light of day.
Siddharth Goswami, lost in the haze,
Searching for truth through the fog and the
maze.

Have you ever felt a sudden, sharp light,
Pierce through the fog of a long, weary night?
A moment of clarity, so vivid and bright,
That it turns the darkest confusion to light?

In the murk of life's tangled threads,
Do you see the glimmers where
understanding spreads?
These veiled moments of clarity, hidden from
view,
Reveal the essence of what's really true.

I recall times when doubts were my guide,
Wandering through the mist, with nowhere to
hide.
Then, like a beacon through the thickening
gloom,
A sudden insight would banish the doom.

Do you cherish these rare flashes of grace,
That come unbidden, a gentle embrace?
In the chaos of living, where answers seem
small,
These moments of clarity, they conquer it all.

When the path ahead seems shrouded and
wide,
Do you wait for the clarity to turn the tide?
Or do you forge ahead through the veiled
unknown,
Hoping for insight that's yet to be shown?

Have you ever felt a shift so profound,
In the midst of confusion, where answers are
found?
These sudden revelations, so clear and so
deep,
Turn the tides of our soul, while the shadows
sleep.

I've walked through the fog, where clarity's
rare,
And glimpsed at the truth through the mist
in the air.
In those fleeting moments, where
understanding ignites,
I've found the strength to confront the nights.

Do you find solace in these rare moments of
truth,
That pierce through the confusion of age and
youth?
Or do you question their origin, their place,
In the grand design, in the infinite space?

The veiled moments of clarity, they come and
they go,
Like stars in the night, with a brilliant, soft
glow.
In the dance of existence, they provide us
with grace,
Illuminating the shadows that darken our
space.

Have you ever felt your heart shift and sway,
In the sudden illumination of a hidden way?
These moments are precious, fleeting and
bright,
Guiding us gently from darkness to light.

As Siddharth Goswami, I ponder and see,
How these moments of clarity shape who we
be.
In the confusion of life, they shine like a star,
Guiding us forward, no matter how far.

What revelations have you found in your
quest,
In the veiled moments that put your mind to
the test?
Do they comfort you, challenge you, or bring
peace,
In the journey of life, where questions never
cease?

In the midst of the fog, when clarity's near,
Do you seize the insight, or let it disappear?
These moments are treasures, so rare and so
bright,
They guide us through darkness and into the
light.

So, let us embrace these moments that come,
As Siddharth Goswami, I find they are some
Of the deepest insights that life can bestow,
Revealing the truths we are meant to know.

What do these veiled moments of clarity
mean to you,
In the journey of life, where the old meets the
new?
Are they guiding stars in the night's silent
song,
Or fleeting glimpses of truths known all
along?

In the quest for meaning, where shadows
retreat,
Embrace these moments when clarity's sweet.
For in the veiled moments of insight and
grace,
We find the answers that light up our space.

Chapter 10. Hidden Lessons in Failure

In the silence of my stumbles, my fall,
Where echoes of failure through shadows call,
I've found the essence of wisdom's grace,
In every misstep, a truth to embrace.

Have you felt the sting of loss so deep,
When dreams slip away, no longer to keep?
In those moments of pain, sharp and real,
What hidden truths do you start to feel?

I've walked with failure, cold as the night,
Yet in its grasp, found courage to fight.
Is failure a shadow, dark and long,
Or the first note of a brighter song?

In the midst of my struggles, I've found,
A lesson carved, so deep and profound.
When the world seems to falter and sway,
What does failure teach you, in its own way?

Through the trials I've faced, I now see,
Failure's threads weave a tapestry.
A pattern rich, with wisdom steeped,
Of lessons that in my heart I keep.

Have you ever wondered about your road,
When failure's whispers make you slow?
In those moments of doubt and fear,
What truths about yourself appear?

Failure's a teacher, though stern it may seem,
Guiding our journey, like a flowing stream.
Do you find strength in despair's cruel grip,
Or struggle to grasp the lessons it slips?

In broken dreams once shining bright,
I've found a fire, burning with might.
What hidden strengths do you ignite,
In the shadows where failure dims the light?

I've known the sting of a heart laid bare,
But through setbacks, learned how to repair.
Do you see failure as a foe or friend,
In the journey that has no clear end?

With every stumble, every fall,
I've learned to rise, to stand tall.
What insights do you gather from your scars,
In the vast, uncharted sea of stars?

Through failure's lens, I've seen the truth,
That growth emerges from the proof.
In lessons learned, do you find peace,
When your spirit feels the heat, seeking
release?

In every fall, a seed is laid,
Where wisdom grows from mistakes we've
made.
Do you embrace these teachings with grace,
Or struggle to find their hidden place?

I've learned that failure is not the end,
But a guide on which we depend.
What role does failure play in your quest,
For wisdom and strength, put to the test?

With each fall, I've risen anew,
Finding wisdom in the struggles I've been
through.
How do you view the trials that come your
way,
In the journey of life, day by day?

Failure's embrace can be tough to bear,
Yet in its shadow, lessons are there.
Do you treasure the growth that comes with
strife,
Or struggle to see through the trials of life?

I've learned that failure's tender touch,
Leads to a grace that means so much.
Do you find solace in lessons that burn,
Or long for the triumphs you've yet to earn?

In the furnace of setbacks, strength is found,
A power that lifts you from the ground.
What secret gifts does failure bestow,
In the tale of your life, only you can know?

Through every failure, I've learned to see,
The hidden lessons that shape me.
Do you find growth in the lessons
hard-earned,
Or struggle to see what you've discerned?

In the tapestry of life's grand design,
Failure's lessons intertwine.
What truths have you uncovered in your
strife,
That guide you through the journey of life?

I've come to cherish each misstep and fall,
For in their shadows, wisdom calls.
What lessons does failure teach you, dear
friend,
In the ever-unfolding story that never ends?

Chapter 11. Unspoken Truths of Love

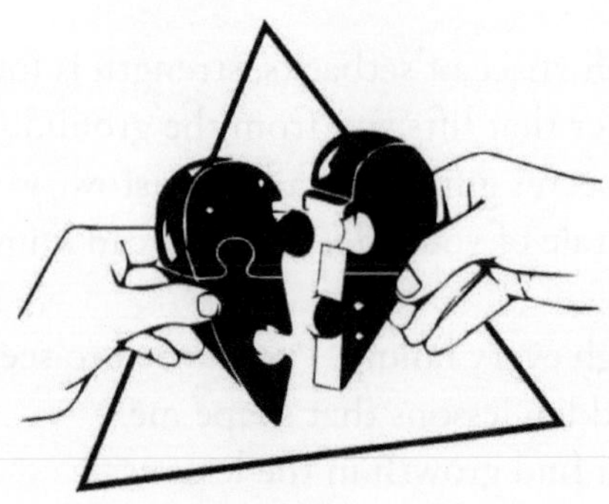

In the quiet spaces between our breaths,
Where love lingers, unspoken, beneath,
I've wandered through the silent fields,
Where emotion's depth quietly yields.

Have you felt the silence that love creates,
In the moments where our heart resonates?
In the hush that follows a tender glance,
What hidden truths in silence dance?

I've felt the weight of words left unsaid,
In the quiet moments shared in bed.
Do you see the love in the quiet eyes,
Where the loudest truths are not disguised?

In the unvoiced whispers of the night,
I've found love's pure and quiet light.
Do you hear the unspoken vows,
In the spaces where our heart allows?

I've learned that love's true depth is shown,
In the silent acts and gestures known.
What does love reveal in its quiet grace,
In the moments of a tender embrace?

The truth of love is often veiled,
In the gentle touches that never failed.
Do you feel the strength in the silence shared,
In the spaces where true feelings are bared?

In the pauses that our hearts can feel,
I've discovered love's true appeal.
What unspoken truths does your heart
convey,
In the silent words that softly sway?

I've found that love's true voice is soft,
In the moments when we drift aloft.
Do you sense the love in the quiet sigh,
In the moments that pass us by?

In the hidden corners of our touch,
I've learned that love means so much.

What truths are found in the silence you
keep,
In the quiet depths where emotions sleep?

I've seen love bloom in the space between,
Where words are few, and feelings keen.
What do you discover in the silent gaze,
In the tender, unspoken praise?

In the stillness of our shared time,
I've felt love's rhythm, slow and prime.
Do you see the love in the silent chords,
In the soft, unspoken words?

In the echoes of our quiet moments,
I've seen the truths that love often presents.
What unspoken words does your heart hide,
In the silent waves where emotions collide?

I've found that love speaks loudest in peace,
In the quiet moments where tensions cease.
What secrets of love do you uncover,
In the silence shared with another?

In the whispers of the night's embrace,
I've seen the silent truths we chase.
Do you find meaning in the silent space,
In the gentle warmth of a tender face?

Through the unspoken and the still,
I've learned that love's truths can thrill.
What does love teach you in its quiet plea,
In the silent dance between you and me?

In the hidden depths of our calm,
I've found that love is a soothing balm.
What silent truths does your heart reveal,
In the quiet places where love is real?

In the silence that our hearts can keep,
I've found love's secrets hidden deep.
What unspoken truths shape your love's view,
In the silent spaces shared by two?

In the quiet moments, soft and pure,
I've found that love's depth can endure.
What hidden meanings does your love
embrace,
In the silent echoes of its grace?

I've seen love's truth in the gentle sigh,
In the spaces where we quietly lie.
What does love reveal in the silent hours,
In the gentle unfolding of its powers?

In the silent dance of our heart's refrain,
I've learned that love's truths remain.
What unspoken stories does your love tell,

In the quiet where its whispers dwell?

In the spaces between our breaths,
I've found love's silent, deep depths.
What does love show in its quiet way,
In the tender moments where silence stays?

Through the quiet of our shared days,
I've learned that love's truth often sways.
What silent revelations does your love hold,
In the quiet moments, warm and bold?

Chapter 12. The Concealed Beauty of Imperfection

In the mirror's gaze, where flaws reveal,
I've found the truth that time can seal.
Are imperfections truly flaws?
Or hidden beauty in nature's laws?

I've learned through years, in trial and test,
That imperfections are what make us blessed.
Do you see the grace in each mistake,
In every flaw, in every break?

In my journey, I've seen the light,
In the shadows of my own slight.

Have you found strength in the cracks you
bear,
In the moments you thought none would
care?

I've seen the beauty in a scar's line,
In the marks that make our stories shine.
What does your heart say about the flaws you
hide,
In the imperfections you try to deny?

In the struggles that life does bestow,
I've found that flaws help us to grow.
Do you recognize the power in your strain,
In the moments that cause you pain?

Through every misstep and every fall,
I've learned to rise and stand tall.
What hidden strengths do you find in your
slip,
In the ways your dreams may trip?

I've embraced the cracks that mar my face,
For they tell the story of my grace.
What hidden beauty lies in the parts of you,
That you wish were different, but are true?

In the imperfections of my soul's song,
I've found where I truly belong.

Do you see the strength in the flaws you show,
In the unique way your true self glows?

I've come to cherish each small defect,
For they reflect the love we protect.
What does your heart reveal about the
imperfections you hide,
In the quiet moments where your true self
resides?

In the way the world sees us as less,
I've found beauty in our soft distress.
What does your spirit tell about the flaws you
face,
In the silent, sacred space?

I've seen perfection in the very cracks,
In the way we mend and never lack.
What strengths are hidden in your pain and
strife,
In the challenges that shape your life?

In the tender moments of our brokenness,
I've discovered love's true finesse.
What does your story tell about the parts that
are torn,
In the beauty of a heart reborn?

I've learned to see the art in the scar,
In the way we shine, both near and far.
What does your journey show about
embracing the flawed,
In the moments where you're awed?

In every error and every tear,
I've found that flaws are something dear.
What do you uncover in your imperfect self,
In the silent strength that you've felt?

I've learned to find the grace in each line,
In the way we grow, and redefine.
What does your heart reveal about the beauty
in the flawed,
In the love that's truly awed?

In the quiet of our imperfections' embrace,
I've found the truth in every trace.
What does your spirit say about the hidden
grace,
In the flaws that time cannot erase?

In the tender moments where we fall,
I've learned that imperfection is our call.
What do you discover in the flaws you own,
In the beauty of a heart fully shown?

Through every challenge, through every scar,
I've found perfection in who we are.
What hidden beauty do you see in your
flawed view,
In the love that comes from being true?

I've come to cherish each imperfection's part,
For they reveal the beauty of the heart.
What does your story say about the flaws you
bear,
In the journey of self-love, rare and fair?

In the concealed beauty of our every flaw,
I've learned to see the love we draw.
What truths do you uncover in the
imperfections you face,
In the silent grace of a heart's embrace?

Chapter 13. Mysteries of
the Inner Self

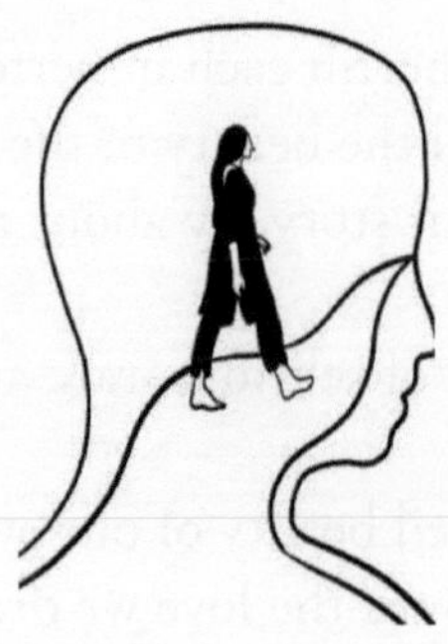

In the quiet chambers of my soul's retreat,
I wander through corridors both dark and
sweet.
What secrets lie behind these veiled doors,
In the depths where no one explores?

I've delved into the shadows of my mind,
Seeking truths that are seldom kind.
Do you hear the whispers of your own
despair,
In the silence where you lay bare?

I've faced the mirror and seen my flaws,
The cracks in the façade, the hidden cause.

What hidden fears do you confront each
night,
In the shadows where you seek the light?

In the labyrinth of my thoughts, I tread,
Through memories and dreams long dead.
What secrets hide in the recesses of your
heart,
In the places where you fall apart?

I've felt the weight of unspoken fears,
The silent echoes of forgotten years.
Do you sense the depth of your hidden pain,
In the moments where you try in vain?

In the darkened corners of my psyche's hold,
I've uncovered stories left untold.
What mysteries dwell in your soul's embrace,
In the quiet, sacred space?

I've encountered doubts that cloud my view,
In the search for a self that feels true.
What truths do you uncover in your own
strife,
In the quest for meaning in your life?

In the depths of my own introspective sea,
I've learned to embrace the parts of me.

What do you discover when you face your
fears,
In the journey through your inner spheres?

I've seen the masks that I wear so well,
The personas I create, the stories I tell.
What masks do you don in your daily dance,
In the ways you seek to enhance?

In the echoes of my own solitude,
I've found the essence of my attitude.
What do you learn from the silence you keep,
In the moments where you silently weep?

I've uncovered layers of my hidden self,
In the depths where I store my mental wealth.
What do you find in the depths of your soul,
In the quest to feel whole?

In the chambers where my fears reside,
I've learned to let go and not to hide.
What fears do you face in your heart's core,
In the moments where you explore?

I've felt the pull of unresolved pain,
The weight of choices that remain.
What unresolved conflicts linger in your
mind,
In the search for peace you hope to find?

In the quiet reflection of my own being,
I've seen the truths that go unseen.
What truths does your heart reveal in its own
song,
In the place where you truly belong?

I've explored the depths of my own design,
Seeking meaning in the intertwine.
What mysteries do you unravel in your quest,
In the search for your inner rest?

In the ebb and flow of my own emotion,
I've found a deep, unspoken devotion.
What does your journey say about the self you
seek,
In the moments that make you unique?

I've faced the storm within my soul's sea,
In the search for what I'm meant to be.
What storms rage within your own mind's
view,
In the depths where your spirit renews?

In the whispers of my deepest night,
I've found fragments of my inner light.
What fragments of truth do you find in your
quest,
In the journey to understand your best?

I've danced with the shadows of my own
fears,
And found wisdom through my tears.
What wisdom do you gain from the darkness
you see,
In the journey to be truly free?

In the silent depths of my inner space,
I've discovered a sacred place.
What does your soul reveal in its quiet plea,
In the search for your true identity?

I've seen the beauty in the hidden part,
In the depths of the human heart.
What beauty do you find in your own quest,
In the search for what you love best?

I've learned that within the hidden shade,
Lies the essence of the self we've made.
What does your journey through the self
reveal,
In the way your heart starts to heal?

In the quest for truths that lie within,
I've learned to embrace both loss and win.
What does your inner world show about the
self you know,
In the journey where your true self grows?

In the deepest reaches of my inner space,
I've found the truth of my own grace.
What does your own search reveal about who
you are,
In the quest to reach for your own star?

In the quiet depth of my self's embrace,
I've found a gentle, sacred place.
What does your soul discover in the journey
deep,
In the secrets your heart keeps?

Chapter 14. Secrets in the Silence of Nature

In the hush of dawn, where whispers are still,
I find my heart is quiet, my thoughts become still.
In nature's silence, I begin to hear,
The secrets that the world holds dear.

I walk through the forest where shadows play,
Feeling the peace in the break of day.
In every leaf and every sound,
I sense the mysteries that abound.

The river's murmur, the wind's soft sigh,
Speak truths that words cannot deny.
Here in nature's calm embrace,
I discover truths in this sacred place.

The mountain's grandeur, the sky's wide span,
Unveil the mysteries of where I am.
In their silence, I see my own,
Reflected in the world I've known.

I sit by the lake where ripples drift,
And ponder the secrets that silence lifts.
In the stillness of the water's face,
I find a moment of gentle grace.

As sunlight filters through the trees,
I feel the quiet bring me ease.
In the hush, my spirit finds,
A deeper peace within my mind.

The quietude of a snowy field,
To my restless heart, a solace yields.
In the stillness of the snowy land,
I grasp the truth with an open hand.

In the evening's calm, as shadows blend,
I find the answers that nature sends.
The silent night, the stars above,
Speak of the wonders of life and love.

In the hush of a solitary hill,
I hear my thoughts become tranquil and still.
The silence teaches, the quiet reveals,
The truth that my heart feels.

The whispering grass, the soft moon's light,
Guide me through the tranquil night.
In the silence, I come to know,
The hidden truths that nature bestows.

I hear the call of a distant bird,
A melody, though it goes unheard.
In the silence, I find a tune,
That dances in the quiet of the moon.

The wind's soft touch upon my face,
Reveals a world of hidden grace.
In nature's silence, I am free,
To see the depths of what can be.

The rustling leaves, the quiet stream,
Hold secrets that surpass the dream.
In the stillness of the forest glade,
I feel the truths that nature made.

The beauty of the sunset's hue,
In silence, takes on a deeper view.
In the twilight's glow, I see the key,
To the mysteries that lie in me.

In the quiet of a starlit night,
I find my soul in a gentle light.
The silence speaks of truths so deep,
In the moments where the world sleeps.

The solitude of the mountain's crest,
Brings to my heart a tranquil rest.
In the vast expanse of the open sky,
I find the answers I can't deny.

As dawn's first light begins to creep,
I find the secrets that silence keeps.
In nature's quiet, I learn to see,
The depths of my own mystery.

The whisper of the wind, the silent call,
In nature's quiet, I find it all.
The secrets of the world unfold,
In the silence that nature holds.

I embrace the stillness, the quiet grace,
And find my truth in nature's face.
In every moment of tranquil peace,
I discover the secrets that never cease.

In the silence of the world so wide,
I find the truths that in me reside.
Nature's quiet is a guiding light,
Revealing secrets in the still of night.

So in the hush of nature's reign,
I find my spirit's deepest gain.
The secrets in the silence clear,
Are the truths that I hold dear.

Through the quiet moments, I am led,
To the wisdom that silence has said.
In nature's embrace, my soul takes flight,
Finding secrets in the silent night.

Chapter 15. The Hidden Patterns of Fate

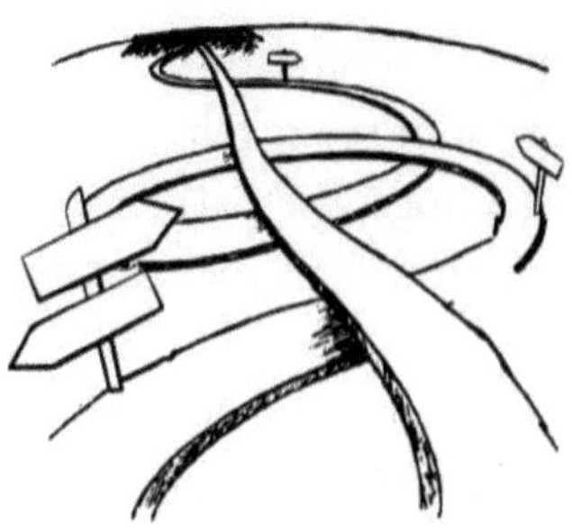

In the tapestry of time, I see the threads,
Woven paths where destiny treads.
Fate's silent patterns, unseen by most,
Guide us gently, like a hidden ghost.

Each twist of fate, a silent dance,
A mystery held in a fleeting glance.
I feel the currents of life's grand stream,
In moments both serene and extreme.

Through the tangled web of chance and
choice,
I hear the echoes of fate's soft voice.
In the crossroads where our paths entwine,
I sense the touch of a hand divine.

As Siddharth Goswami, I trace the lines,
Of fate's design in the grand confines.
In every chance encounter, every twist,
The unseen patterns cannot be dismissed.

I recall the days of serendipity,
When life's random turns felt meant to be.
The chance meetings, the paths we stray,
All reveal the patterns in their own way.

In the quiet moments, the deep reflections,
I uncover fate's hidden connections.
The threads of life, so fine and frail,
Interweave in an intricate tale.

The choices made in shadowed light,
Unveil the patterns hidden from sight.
In every choice, a hidden force,
Guiding us on a preordained course.

I remember nights of deep introspection,
Where destiny's dance felt like a connection.
The stars aligned, the paths diverged,
In the symphony of fate, our lives are surged.

From childhood dreams to grown-up
schemes,
Fate's patterns weave through our wildest
dreams.

In the laughter and in the tears we shed,
The hidden patterns of life are spread.

In the face of trials, in moments of strife,
I see the unseen hand guiding my life.
Through every struggle and every fight,
Fate's patterns emerge in the softest light.

The gentle whispers of chance's breath,
Guide us through the living and through
death.
In every turn and every fate we face,
The hidden patterns of life we trace.

As Siddharth Goswami, I find the grace,
In the unseen patterns that time embrace.
The coincidences, the fortuitous turns,
Reveal the fate that quietly burns.

In every decision, both large and small,
The patterns of fate weave through it all.
The intersections of lives, so profound,
Show how destiny's patterns are bound.

Through life's ebb and flow, we ride the wave,
In the unseen patterns, we find the brave.
The hidden forces that shape our days,
Guide us through the labyrinthine maze.

In quiet reflection, in moments so still,
I uncover the patterns that fate fulfills.
Through the whispers of destiny's art,
I see the hidden patterns of the heart.

In the dance of life, in the grand design,
The hidden patterns of fate align.
Through the chaos and the calm we face,
I find the patterns that time can trace.

So in the pages of human existence,
I seek the hidden patterns of persistence.
As Siddharth Goswami, I unveil the fate,
In the grand design, both small and great.

In every heartbeat, in every breath,
The patterns of fate weave life and death.
Through the mysteries of time and space,
I find the hidden patterns of life's embrace.

Chapter 16. Echoes from Forgotten Places

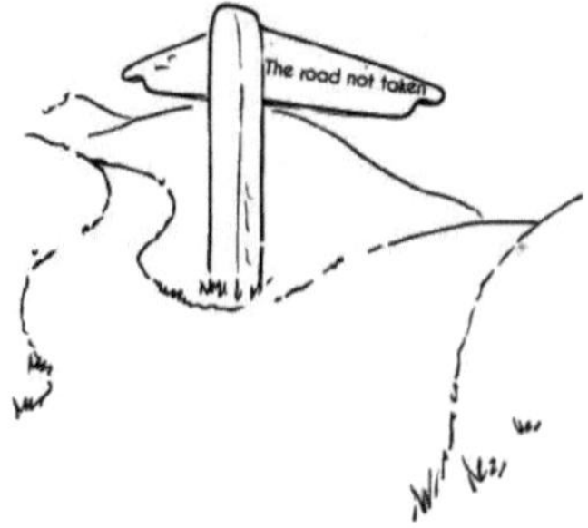

In the quiet corners of the world's embrace,
I find the echoes of forgotten space.
Siddharth Goswami, I tread on paths unseen,
Where memories linger in places once serene.

In abandoned towns where shadows play,
I listen to what the silence has to say.
Old buildings whisper of their faded grace,
Each crack and creak, a story's trace.

I wander through fields where time has
ceased,
Amongst the remnants where memories are
released.
Every rusted gate and every broken wall,
Speaks of the past, of times that call.

In the old library where dust collects,
The books still hold their stories and their
effects.
I read the lines that time has blurred,
In the quiet, forgotten words are heard.

I visit the playgrounds where laughter died,
In swings that sway with the wind's soft
guide.
The echoes of children's joy, now still,
Reverberate through the emptiness, a tranquil
thrill.

In forgotten letters and dusty chests,
I uncover secrets of forgotten quests.
Each piece of paper, each worn-out seam,
Tells of hopes and dreams once deemed
supreme.

In old photographs where smiles are caught,
I see the lives that time has forgot.
Faces frozen in moments of delight,
Now ghostly figures in the fading light.

Through the overgrown paths and weedy
lanes,
I sense the whispers of lost refrains.
Nature's touch turns grandeur to dust,
Transforming human works, as all must.

In the stillness of a vacant room,
Echoes of laughter chase away the gloom.
Every step on the creaking floor,
Tells tales of lives that came before.

I recall dreams that time left behind,
In the hush, they come to mind.
Youthful hopes, once vivid and bold,
Now whisper softly as the night grows cold.

In the remnants of a bustling past,
I find stories of joy that still last.
Faded signs and shattered glass,
Hold whispers of days that have passed.

In the quiet of these forsaken halls,
A touch of lost grace softly calls.
Memories of lives that once were near,
Are etched in silence, crystal clear.

Through dusty halls and cobwebbed beams,
I uncover fragments of lost dreams.
Each forgotten spot holds a piece of the art,
A reflection of the past, a glimpse of the
heart.

I walk through the alleys where time stood
still,
Finding solace in the silence, a tranquil thrill.

The echoes from the past, both loud and clear,
Reveal the stories that I hold dear.

In the whispers of the wind through the trees,
I hear the tales of forgotten pleas.
Each gust of air, each rustling leaf,
Speaks of the past, both joy and grief.

In the abandoned homes where life once
thrived,
I uncover the essence of the lives that
survived.
The echoes of footsteps, the creak of the floor,
Tell the stories of those who lived there
before.

As Siddharth Goswami, I uncover the grace,
In the forgotten places, the hidden space.
The echoes of time, both tender and wise,
Reveal the truths that time defies.

In the quiet of these forgotten lands,
I find the stories that time disbands.
The echoes from the past, so deep and clear,
Guide me to the memories I hold dear.

In every corner where silence resides,
I discover the past where truth abides.
The echoes from forgotten places remain,
A testament to what time cannot contain.

Chapter 17. The Unseen Hands of Time

In the quiet moments, where shadows play,
I sense the unseen hands of time each day.
Siddharth Goswami, I feel its subtle touch,
In the gentle rhythm that means so much.

Time weaves its threads through every seam,
Molding our lives like a sculptor's dream.
In every tick and tock of the clock's embrace,
Time etches its mark on each hidden place.

I walk through the corridors of my past,
Where echoes of moments are bound to last.
In old photographs and letters faded,
Time's touch is subtly created.

The sunrise and sunset, a dance so grand,
Time's power is felt in a fleeting strand.
Each dawn writes a new chapter bright,
Guided by time's unseen light.

Years pass by, and I see the grace,
As time carves out each fleeting space.
From youthful dreams to wisdom's sway,
Time shapes our path in its gentle way.

I recall the laughter from days of yore,
Tears that fell and memories more.
Time's hand, though soft and unseen,
Guides us through what might have been.

In evening's calm and quiet fall,
I hear time's whisper, a gentle call.
It speaks of paths we've walked alone,
And seeds of the future we've sown.

Lines upon my face, I see,
Marks of time's enduring spree.
Each wrinkle tells a story true,
Of how time's hands shaped me and you.

Through the years, I've watched the change,
Time's mysteries are vast, so strange.
From childhood dreams to grown-up stride,
Time's unseen hands are our guide.

Moments slip like sand through seams,
As time's river flows through dreams.
In joy or strife, with every breath,
Time molds the contours of our depth.

In quiet corners of my mind,
Time's traces are soft and kind.
It shapes our hopes, our fears, our thoughts,
Marking the years as we've sought.

Time's touch is subtle but so deep,
In every heartbeat, in every sleep.
It crafts our stories, dreams, and goals,
Etching its mark on our very souls.

In moments still, I pause and see,
How time has shaped both you and me.
Its touch guides us through every day,
Leading us gently on our way.

Changes in the world abound,
Time's hands have made their bound.
From the rise and fall of tides so high,
To the ebb and flow of life's sky.

In every sunrise and each twilight call,
Time's hands are there, silent and tall.
They shape our past, present, and fate,
In ways both subtle and truly great.

As Siddharth Goswami, I ponder and muse,
On time's unseen hand and its gentle cues.
In every tick and every tock,
Time shapes our lives around the clock.

In moments big and moments small,
Time weaves its threads through it all.
Its influence felt in every breath we take,
Guiding our journey, every choice we make.

So as I walk this path of mine,
I sense the touch of time's design.
In every heartbeat and every sigh,
Time's unseen hands guide us as they fly.

In the end, it's time that carves our days,
In its silent, profound, and subtle ways.
Through joy and strife, in every part,
Time's gentle hands mold the essence of our
heart.

Chapter 18. The Secret of Resilience

In the hush of storms where shadows play,
I search for strength each passing day.
Siddharth Goswami, through trials deep,
Finds resilience where doubts might creep.

Resilience is a beacon burning bright,
Leading us through the darkest night.
In struggles fierce and tempests wild,
It is inner strength that helps us rise.

I've trod through valleys, faced my fear,
Seen mountains rise and felt the chill near.
Yet in each struggle, in every fight,
I've discovered a resilient light.

When the world felt heavy, hope seemed thin,
I learned to find my strength within.
Through steepest climbs and hardest trials,
Resilience turned my tears to smiles.

In times of weakness, where shadows play,
Resilience shines and clears the way.
It's quiet courage in despair's dark room,
The gentle whisper that sweeps the gloom.

Through every setback and storm I've braved,
Resilience is the path I've paved.
In each failure, heartache, every tear,
I've found the power to persevere.

Battles within have left their scars,
Yet resilience turned each wound to stars.
In broken places, where pain took hold,
I found the strength to reignite the bold.

In the darkest hours when hope seemed lost,
Resilience showed the price of frost.
It's the courage to move despite the fight,
The steadfast heart that holds the light.

Dreams have crumbled, hopes have waned,
Yet resilience remains unchained.
In every doubt, every fall from grace,
It's inner strength that keeps the pace.

Amid the world's relentless call,
Resilience stands as the strongest wall.
It's bending without breaking apart,
A steady beat of a determined heart.

In life's chapters, where challenges loom,
Resilience is the light that sweeps the gloom.
It's the power to rise after each defeat,
The courage to stand, to never retreat.

Through echoes of time and fate's design,
Resilience has taught that all will be fine.
In moments of silence, between the streams,
I find the strength to chase my dreams.

In every struggle, each challenge faced,
Resilience has been my guiding grace.
It's the silent force that drives my strive,
The inner strength that keeps me alive.

Siddharth Goswami, through each test I see,
Resilience is the key to being truly free.
In every setback, each trial, every pace,
It's the hidden strength that finds its place.

So as I tread this wide life's space,
Resilience is my guiding grace.
Through every storm and trial's quest,
It's the inner strength that grants me rest.

In the secret of resilience, I find my way,
Through the darkest night and the brightest
day.
It's the power within that never fades,
The strength of the heart that always stays.

Chapter 19. Whispers from the Void

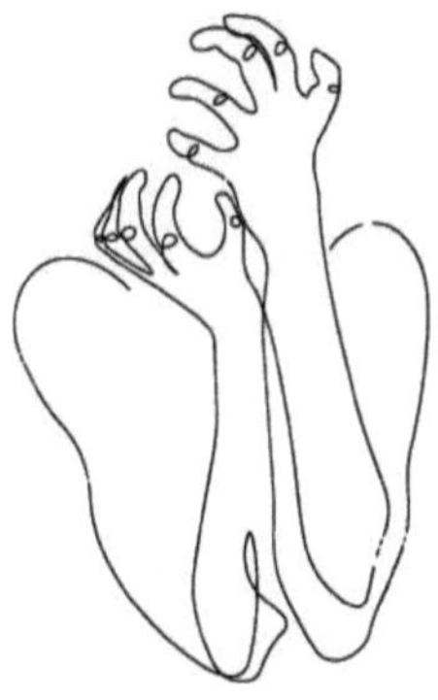

In the depths where silence dwells, a whisper
grows,
From the vast, uncharted void where no light
shows.
Siddharth Goswami here, with thoughts so
wide,
I delve into the emptiness, where shadows
hide.

Have you ever gazed into the abyss so deep,
Where echoes of the unknown silently creep?
In that quiet space where fears are born,
What secrets does the void, so dark, adorn?

I've stared into the void, felt its cold embrace,
And in that emptiness, I found a hidden
place.
A realm where questions dance with ghosts of
old,
And the whispers of the void turn into stories
told.

What is the void, if not a canvas bare,
Waiting for the brush of thoughts to dare?
In the emptiness, we confront our deepest
fears,
And hear the whispers that have lingered for
years.

Is the void a chasm or a mirror clear?
Reflecting our hopes, our doubts, our deepest
tear?
In that silent expanse, I've learned to see,
The echoes of my soul, and what they mean to
me.

When we face the void, we touch the
unknown,
Confronting the intangible, our minds are
shown
That emptiness is not just a void of space,
But a place where our deepest thoughts find
grace.

Through my own journey, I've faced this
empty dome,
Where the void seemed to speak, and I felt at
home.
In moments of despair, when shadows grew
long,
I heard the whispers of the void, a silent song.

In murmurs soft and shadows bright,
The void speaks both by day and night.
It asks us questions, deep and grand,
And guides us through where fears disband.

Have you felt its chilling grace,
When darkness wraps its cold embrace?
In silence deep, a truth is found,
In whispers where our answers sound.

The void's not just a place of dread,
But where our clearest insights spread.
It's a realm where we confront our core,
And find the courage to explore.

When the void calls, it's not to fright,
But to stir our hearts and shed new light.
In emptiness, our deepest self we face,
And find the strength we have in place.

What lies beyond this empty sea?
Is it where dreams and hopes roam free?

I've pondered these as I journeyed through,
And found the void reveals our essence true.

In emptiness, though fear might loom,
We find what's rare and banish gloom.
The whispers of the void, though not always
kind,
Guide us to truths we seek to find.

Have you felt that silent, vast embrace,
Where void's whispers leave their trace?
In stillness, courage comes to be,
As the void mirrors back to me.

Siddharth Goswami, through my quest,
I've learned the void reveals our best.
In silence, midst the quiet calls,
We find the strength within our walls.

So ponder well the void's dark might,
It's both shadowed depth and guiding light.
In whispers of the void, a path you'll find,
Leading you to truths that lie behind.

Embrace the silence, let its whispers show,
For in the void, our true selves grow.
Through Siddharth's journey, may you see,
The whispers of the void, and who you're
meant to be.

Chapter 20. The Hidden Symphony of Life

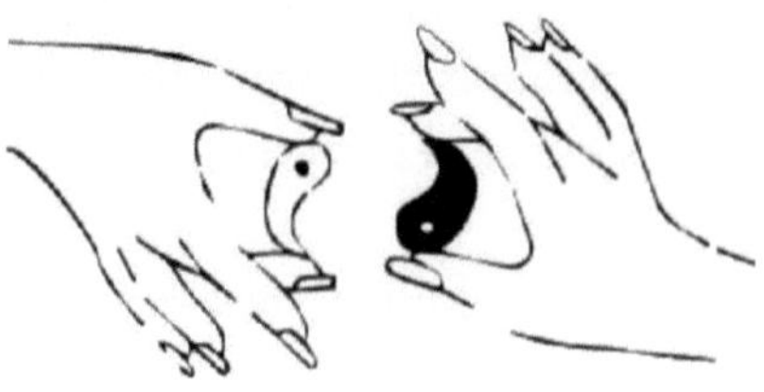

In quiet moments when the world is still,
A melody emerges, a heart's sweet thrill.
I'm Siddharth Goswami, in tune with the
unseen,
Guiding you through rhythms where magic
lies between.

Have you felt the pulse of life so grand,
Where every beat is touched by an unseen
hand?
In chaos and calm, a hidden tune is played,
A symphony of life from dawn till twilight's
fade.

Through moonlit silence, I've wandered deep,
Heard the harmony in the night's gentle
sweep.

In solitude's embrace, where the world drifts
away,
I've sensed the music that stars softly convey.

What if life's rhythm is more than we know?
A dance of moments that we scarcely show?
In each day's ebb and flow, a secret song is
spun,
A melody of being known by everyone.

Have you seen how seasons shift their tone,
From spring's whispers to winter's cold zone?
In every cycle, a profound beat is found,
A hidden symphony in the world's grand
sound.

In my life's journey, notes align with grace,
In joy and sorrow, moments interlace.
Through trials and triumphs, a rhythm plays
on,
A melody of life that is never truly gone.

Do you hear whispers of a hidden score,
In rustling leaves or the ocean's roar?
In children's laughter or a lover's sigh,
A harmony lifts the heart to the sky.

Life's intricate art reveals a symphony's heart,
Touching every soul, a masterpiece of art.

From atoms small to cosmic sweeps,
A rhythm of existence in our waking and
sleep.

The hidden symphony isn't always clear,
But felt in moments we hold dear.
At dawn's quiet or night's gentle hush,
A melody finds its way through the silent
blush.

Have you wondered about the rhythm in your
days,
In routine's hum or extraordinary ways?
A song weaves through each breath we take,
A life's harmony that no end can break.

In still forests or bustling streets,
I hear a symphony so sweet.
In the world's turn and our daily lives,
A melody the universe freely provides.

Have you sensed peace in chaos profound,
Or beauty in silence where no sound is found?
In existence's ebb and flow, a secret revealed,
A hidden symphony, beautifully concealed.

In my journey, I've learned to hear the
unheard,
World's whispers, unspoken word.

Through ups and downs, the rhythm stays,
A song of life flowing through joys and gray
days.

The hidden symphony is a dance of time,
A melody both simple and sublime.
In every heartbeat and each breath we take,
A rhythm of existence that all partake.

So as you ponder the music that lies beneath,
In the quiet of your soul, or in the world's
deep wreath,
Know that the hidden symphony is a guide so
true,
A melody of life that's waiting just for you.

Siddharth Goswami here, with a song to
share,
Of the hidden harmony that's always there.
In the tapestry of existence, the rhythm is
clear,
A symphony of life that we hold dear.

Chapter 21. The Echoes of Unsaid Words

In the quiet of the morning, when the world
is still asleep,
I think of all the words I've left unsaid, buried
deep.
What if I had spoken up? What if you had
heard?
Would things be different now, if I had shared
each word?

Every glance that went unnoticed, every
touch that wasn't felt,
Are like whispers in the wind, or snowflakes
that quietly melt.
Do you ever think of moments that you wish
you could reclaim?
Do you wonder what I thought, when I didn't
call your name?

In the spaces between us, where silence softly
lies,
There are echoes of the words we never
vocalized.
Sometimes they are soft and gentle, like a
tender sigh,
Other times they scream so loud, I'm afraid to
even try.

Have you ever felt the weight of something
left unsaid,
A knot within your stomach, a heaviness in
your head?
I've often sat in darkness, just listening to my
heart,
Feeling every beat and wondering where to
start.

We've walked on roads divergent, yet parallel,
it seems,
Your laughter echoes in my mind, like
snippets from my dreams.
Do you feel the same way, or am I alone in
this maze?
Are there things you wished you'd told me,
back in those bright days?

I remember when I saw you, standing by the
sea,
I wanted to tell you how much you meant to
me.
But words got caught behind my lips, held
prisoner in my mouth,
And all that came out was silence, as vast as
the south.

The weight of unsaid words can pull a person
down,
Can change the path they're walking, can
make them almost drown.
Yet sometimes, in this silence, there's a truth
we must embrace,
The things we choose to leave unsaid are part
of our own grace.

Do you think about our silence; does it haunt
your dreams?
Do you wonder about my thoughts, like I
wonder about your schemes?
In the space between each heartbeat, in the
pause before the dawn,
There's a world of words unsaid that I've been
dwelling on.

I've seen the light in your eyes, and I've felt
your warm embrace,
But the words I never spoke have left an
empty space.
Have you felt it too, that longing, that silent,
aching need?
Do you understand my silence; do you see it
as a creed?

Sometimes I wonder if we're all just shadows
on the wall,
Dancing in the firelight, afraid to risk a fall.
What would happen, do you think, if we
spoke all our fears?
Would the world keep turning, would we
shed all our tears?

Each morning brings a new chance, a fresh
breath of air,
To speak the words we're holding, to let go of
our despair.
But sometimes we just can't, and we never
really know why,
Maybe it's because some things are better left
to die.

The unsaid words, they linger, like ghosts that
never fade,
They wrap around my heartstrings, in silence,
I'm betrayed.

Yet there's a strange comfort in them, like a
friend who never leaves,
In the echoes of unsaid words, I find the
strength to grieve.

What are the words you've left unsaid? What
truths are you afraid to tell?
Do they weigh upon your shoulders, like an
anchor or a bell?
Have you found peace in silence, or does it
drive you mad?
Do you wish you'd said "I love you" to
someone who made you glad?

I look out at the horizon, where the sky meets
the sea,
And I think of all the things that you've never
said to me.
But in that vast expanse of blue, I see hope in
every wave,
That one day we might find the words, and be
brave.

In every life, there are moments, when silence
speaks so loud,
When words are just too heavy, when hearts
are just too proud.
But maybe, in that silence, there's a story to
be told,

Of love and loss and yearning, of hearts that
still unfold.

Have you ever felt the echo of a word you
couldn't say?
Has it haunted you in darkness, does it haunt
you still today?
I know that I have struggled, I've fought with
every breath,
To find the courage to speak up, to conquer
fear of death.

But still, the words remain, like stars upon
the night,
They twinkle in the distance, they shimmer
just out of sight.
And I wonder if you feel them, if you know
they're there,
Or if the words I never said just vanish into
air.

In the end, we are all stories, written with
unsaid words,
With chapters that remain unread, like flocks
of silent birds.
But perhaps, in our silence, there's something
we can find,
A deeper understanding, a peace within the
mind.

So, I'll keep my secrets close, and I'll treasure
every word,
For sometimes in the quiet, the loudest voice
is heard.
And I'll look up at the stars, and I'll whisper
to the night,
The words I never said to you, the truths I
couldn't write.

And now, dear reader, it's your turn to share
your hidden tales,
To whisper in the darkness, to lift the heavy
veils.
For in the echo of unsaid words, there's a
world that's yet to be,
A place where every silent voice can finally be
free.

I am Siddharth Goswami, a poet and a
dreamer too,
Writing words unspoken, hoping they reach
you.
In every line and verse, in every thought and
rhyme,
I search for truth and beauty, across the sands
of time.

Chapter 22. The Forgotten Rhythms of Childhood

In the quiet corners of my mind, where the shadows softly fall,
I wander back to childhood days, where I stood so small.
Do you remember the mornings, when the world felt so grand?
When the sun kissed our cheeks and we played in the sand?

Back then, life was simple, filled with laughter and cheer,
The worries of the world were something we didn't fear.
Have you ever wished to go back, to those days so carefree?
To relive the moments when our spirits soared free?

I think of the games we played, under the
wide-open sky,
Running wild through fields, feeling as if we
could fly.
Do you recall the taste of rain, fresh upon our
tongues?
Or the joy of finding treasures, like rocks and
shells among?

The world seemed endless then, a place of
wonder and awe,
Where every new discovery left us speechless
and in awe.
Have you ever stopped to think, what
happened to that joy?
Where did we lose the magic, the dreams we
had as a boy?

I remember the sound of my mother's call,
echoing through the air,
As the day turned to dusk and the stars began
to flare.
Did your mother call you too, when the light
began to fade?
Did you feel the warmth of home, in every
meal she made?

Those were days of innocence, where
everything was bright,
When fears were just shadows, fading into the
night.
Do you sometimes close your eyes and let
your mind take flight?
To those golden days of childhood, when
everything felt right?

I recall the friends I had, their faces clear as
day,
We shared our dreams and secrets, in the
games we used to play.
Do you remember your friends, their laughter
loud and bold?
Do you wonder where they are now, as the
years have slowly rolled?

In those days, every moment was a story to be
told,
Adventures in our backyards, mysteries to
unfold.
Have you ever told your children, the tales of
your youth?
Do you think they'd understand, or see it as
the truth?

I still remember the summers, long and hot
and free,
The smell of grass and daisies, the buzz of a
honeybee.
Do you miss the warmth of summer, the joy
of being wild?
Do you yearn for the freedom, that we knew
as a child?

The rhythm of my childhood, beats softly in
my chest,
A melody of memories, of times I loved the
best.
Can you hear the rhythm too, in the quiet of
the night?
Does it bring a tear to your eye, or fill you
with delight?

Sometimes I visit places, that I knew when I
was small,
Hoping to find the echoes, that linger in my
soul's hall.
Do you visit your old haunts, where you
played and laughed?
Do you feel the same longing, for the
moments that have passed?

In every old playground, in every tree I see,
I find pieces of my childhood, calling out to
me.
Have you ever found a place, that felt like
yours?
Where time seemed to stand still, beyond
life's closing doors?

There were days of endless wonder, of
climbing every hill,
Of chasing after rainbows, and dreams to
fulfill.
Do you chase your dreams now, with the same
youthful zest?
Or have the years made you weary, put your
dreams to rest?

I think of the lessons learned, in games of
hide and seek,
The joy of being found, the thrill of the
mystique.
Did you learn those lessons too, in the
playgrounds of your youth?
Did they shape the person you've become,
your kindness and your truth?

In the books I used to read, filled with
dragons and knights,
I found the courage to face my fears, to stand
up for my rights.
Do you still read those stories, do they make
your heart race?
Do they remind you of the hero, you once
wanted to embrace?

The years have moved so quickly, like leaves
upon the breeze,
But the memories of childhood still put my
mind at ease.
Do you hold your memories close, as treasures
deep inside?
Do they bring a smile to your lips, or tears
that you hide?

I think of my father's voice, strong and sure
and wise,
And the way he taught me to see the world,
through hopeful eyes.
Did your father guide you too, with wisdom
soft and clear?
Did his words shape your journey, did they
calm your deepest fear?

The innocence of childhood, it fades as we
grow,
But the lessons that we learned, still in our
hearts, they glow.
Do you hold on to that innocence, does it
guide your way?
Do you let it lead you, in the decisions you
make each day?

As I look back on those days, with a heart full
of pride,
I see the path I've walked, the distance in my
stride.
Do you see your journey too, in the light of
your past?
Do you cherish every moment, knowing they
don't last?

And so, I ask you, reader, to think of your
own youth,
To remember the days of wonder, of laughter,
and of truth.
Can you feel the rhythm now, of the child you
used to be?
Do you hear it echo softly, through the
branches of a tree?

Let us not forget the child, who lives within
us still,
The one who knew no limits, who climbed
every hill.
Do you let that child guide you, when the
days grow long?
Do you find strength in their spirit, when the
world feels wrong?

For in the rhythms of childhood, there lies a
secret key,
A way to unlock the joy, the person we were
meant to be.
Will you take a moment now, to dance to that
old tune?
Will you let the child within you, beneath the
pale moon?

The memories of youth, they whisper soft and
low,
In every laugh and every tear, in every joy and
woe.
Will you let them guide you, as you walk your
path ahead?
Will you cherish every moment, before they
too are shed?

So here's to the child within us, to the rhythm
of our days,
To the laughter and the tears, to the games
and the plays.
Will you join me on this journey, as we turn
the pages anew?
Will you share your story too, and let your
voice ring true?

For I am Siddharth Goswami, a poet with a
heart,
I write of all our stories, the whole and every
part.
In every word I pen, in every line I weave,
I hope to capture moments; the memories we
grieve.

Do you feel the rhythm now, in the beating of
your heart?
Does it take you back to childhood, where
every day was a brand-new start?
Let's embrace those forgotten days, and hold
them close tonight,
For in the forgotten rhythms, we find our
truest light.

Chapter 23. Unveiling the Mask of Society

In this world, we all wear masks so fine,
Crafted with care, like a poet's rhyme.
But behind this veil, who do we find?
Is it truly us, or shadows entwined?

Siddharth, my name, like a whispered song,
In this journey of life, where do we belong?
I've walked these roads, so many times before,
But each step hides more, more, and more.

Society's gaze, ever sharp, ever keen,
Judging our acts, what we say, what we mean.
Do you feel the weight of those unseen eyes?
Watching, waiting, for the truth in our lies?

I've felt it too, that pressure to conform,
To fit the mold, to weather the storm.
But tell me, dear reader, have you ever dared,
To remove that mask, to stand up, bare?

In moments of silence, when the world is
asleep,
Do you hear your heart; does it speak deep?
What does it say, when it's just you and the
night,
Does it cry out, or does it ignite?

I've asked myself these questions in the dark,
And found that truth leaves a burning mark.
Do we chase approval, or do we seek peace?
Is it love we crave, or just sweet release?

The mask I wore, it fit so well,
But underneath, it became my hell.
Have you ever felt trapped, by your own
disguise?
Wishing, hoping, for a life without lies?

Siddharth Goswami, a name I wear with
pride,
Yet I wonder, who am I, when I step inside?
Do you ponder the same, my friend, in your
day?
What truths in you, do you hide away?

Let's walk this path together, you and I,
Let's question, let's wonder, let's even defy.
For in these lines, there's more than just
rhyme,
There's a call to be real, to reclaim our time.

So, take off your mask, if only for a while,
And look in the mirror, greet your own smile.
What do you see, when the facade is gone?
Is it someone you know, or a stranger at
dawn?

I've peeled away layers, with each passing
year,
And found in the end, there's nothing to fear.
But to get there, the journey is long,
Filled with doubts, and questions so strong.

Siddharth, I write, with an open heart,
Tell me, dear reader, where do you start?
What stories lie buried beneath your skin?
What battles are fought, where you never
win?

In the quiet moments, when the world is still,
Do you find peace, or do you feel the chill?
These are the questions that haunt us all,
Yet in the search, we begin to stand tall.

So, join me now, as we lift the veil,
As we break the silence, as we tell the tale.
Of lives unmasked, of hearts set free,
This is our story, yours and mine.

Together we'll find, what's hidden inside,
In the pages of life, where secrets reside.
Siddharth Goswami, a name that's mine,
But the journey we share, is yours and divine.

Now ask yourself, and be sincere,
What is it you seek, what do you fear?
For in this world, where masks are worn,
True freedom lies in being reborn.

So let's walk this road, till the very end,
With open hearts, as both lover and friend.
For the masks we shed, and the truths we
find,
Will forever change both heart and mind.

And as you read, as these words sink deep,
May they stir your soul; may they make you
weep.
But more than that, may they make you see,
The beauty in truth, the power in "me."

Chapter 24. Secrets of the Celestial Dance

Beneath the sky, so vast and wide,
I gaze at stars, where secrets hide.
They whisper tales of time and space,
Of cosmic journeys and endless race.

Have you ever wondered, dear friend,
Where do these stars begin, or end?
Do they shine for us, as we sleep,
Guarding our dreams, their mysteries deep?

I once sat alone, beneath the night,
The moon was full, the stars were bright.
I felt so small, in that grand expanse,
Caught in the rhythm of a celestial dance.

The Milky Way stretched far and far,
A river of light, each tiny star.
I thought of you, and what you'd say,
If you could see the heavens play.

Do you think we're just a fleeting spark,
In this universe, so vast and dark?
Or are we, like stars, meant to shine,
To leave a mark, a sacred sign?

In the silence, I heard the night,
It spoke to me in soft, soft light.
"Siddharth," it said, "Do you see?
You are a part of this mystery."

I felt a pull, a gentle sway,
As if the stars led me away.
To places where time is but a thread,
Woven into what lies ahead.

Have you felt the weight of the sky,
Pressed upon your soul, as you lie?
Watching, waiting, for some sign,
That we are not alone, but divine?

I saw a comet, streaking fast,
A fiery dancer, from the past.
I thought, could it be, you and me,
Caught in this dance, eternally?

What stories do these stars conceal,
What hidden truths will they reveal?
Are we their echoes, lost in time,
Or are we just another rhyme?

I've stood on mountains, touched the sea,
But nothing compares to what could be.
In the cosmos, I see a chance,
To understand this timeless dance.

Have you stood in awe, in pure delight,
Beneath the tapestry of the night?
Wondered if there's more to this,
Than just a life of pain and bliss?

Stars align and drift apart,
Much like matters of the heart.
Do we find our way by fate,
Or do we choose our cosmic state?

In this dance, there is no end,
Just twists and turns, that bend and blend.
And in this vast, eternal flow,
We learn the things we need to know.

I ask you now, what do you see,
When you look up, where stars run free?
Do you feel their pull, their gentle nudge,
Or are you bound by earth's firm grudge?

I've felt it all, the joy, the pain,
Beneath the starlight's soft refrain.
And as I write, I hope you find,
A piece of peace, in heart and mind.

In every star, a story waits,
A chance for us to contemplate.
The secrets of this cosmic trance,
Unveiling life's celestial dance.

So take my hand, let's journey far,
Beyond the moon, past every star.
For in this vast, unending night,
Together, we can find the light.

And as we dance, in this cosmic groove,
Feel the rhythm, let it soothe.
For in the stars, in you, in me,
Lie the answers to what we seek to be.

Do you hear it now, the universe's hum?
A song of old, yet so young.
In its notes, I find my name,
Siddharth Goswami, one and the same.

Let's end this night with one last glance,
And join once more in the celestial dance.
For we are but stars, shining bright,
Together, we conquer the endless night.

Chapter 25. Beneath the Waves of Emotion

Have you ever stood by the shore,
Felt the waves, heard the ocean's roar?
I often do, lost in deep thought,
Where each wave whispers, a lesson is taught.

I ask myself, "What drives the tide?
Is it the moon, or something inside?"
Do you ever feel the same, my friend?
That emotions flow without an end?

I've felt anger like a stormy sea,
Raging wild, crashing over me.
But then, the calm that follows the fight,
Brings peace, like a gentle night.

Do you know what I mean when I say,
Emotions guide us, they lead the way?
From joy's bright light to sorrow's shade,
In every feeling, a truth is laid.

Sometimes I feel, like waves on sand,
My heart is drawn by an unseen hand.
Have you felt the pull of love's embrace,
Or the sting of loss, its empty space?

I've laughed under the sun's warm glow,
And cried in the rain, letting tears flow.
Each emotion, a wave in this sea,
Tells a story of you, of me.

Do you ever feel a sudden tide,
Of joy or pain you cannot hide?
What do you do when feelings swell,
Do you ride the wave or in it dwell?

I've seen people build walls so high,
To block the waves, to never cry.
But I wonder, don't you too?
If these walls are meant to break through?

Sometimes, I dive deep into my heart,
To find the emotions that set me apart.
In those depths, I find my soul,
Seeking answers to make me whole.

Have you ever swum in the waters clear,
Only to find murky thoughts appear?
What do you do when shadows come?
Do you fight them, or do you run?

In my journey, I've learned to see,
That each wave carries a piece of me.
From childhood dreams to adult fears,
The sea of emotion is filled with tears.

Do you think emotions are a sign,
Of weakness, or of the divine?
I've found strength in the softest cry,
And courage in a long goodbye.

I've walked alone, on moonlit nights,
Talking to stars, seeking their light.
Have you ever asked the sky above,
What it knows of pain and love?

I believe we're all like waves,
Rising, falling, in life's brave maze.
And in this dance, this ebb and flow,
We learn to let our feelings show.

Sometimes, I think of all I've lost,
And wonder, was it worth the cost?
But then I feel a wave of grace,
And find my peace in time's embrace.

Do you find yourself lost at sea,
In the waves of what could be?
Or do you ride with the wind so free,
Embracing life's uncertainty?

I often ask the ocean's edge,
What secrets lie beneath its ledge?
And in return, it sends a wave,
A reminder of the courage I crave.

Have you ever danced in the rain,
Let it wash away the pain?
I find joy in every drop,
Each one a chance to never stop.

To live, to feel, to truly be,
Is to dive deep into the sea.
And though the waves may sometimes scare,
In their depth, I find what's rare.

I am Siddharth, with words I weave,
A tapestry of the truths I believe.
And in these lines, I hope you see,
The waves of emotion that set us free.

So next time you stand by the shore,
Listen closely to the ocean's lore.
For in each wave, there is a song,
A reminder that we all belong.

In this sea, we are not alone,
We share a journey, a path unknown.
And with each step, each breath we take,
We ride the waves, the lives we make.

Chapter 26. The Silent Cry of the Earth

I stand alone beneath the sky so vast,
Feeling the echoes of our planet's past.
Have you ever stopped and listened well,
To the silent stories, the earth can tell?

Each leaf that falls, each whispering breeze,
Is a chapter written in the earth's pleas.
Do you hear it too, this quiet cry?
Or do you look away, let it pass by?

I've walked through forests, lush and green,
Where every tree held secrets unseen.
But now I see, the woods grow thin,
A stark reminder of what we've been.

Do you remember when rivers ran clear,
When the air was fresh, no need to fear?

I think back to those days of old,
And feel a chill, a creeping cold.

I've seen mountains, proud and high,
Now scarred and broken, asking why.
Have you felt the earth beneath your feet,
Begging softly, with a steady beat?

The oceans too, they call out loud,
Waves crashing, like a weeping crowd.
Do you sense the sorrow in their roar,
Or just the splash upon the shore?

I once believed the world would last,
Unchanging, eternal, holding fast.
But now I see the earth in pain,
And wonder, can we heal again?

Do you wonder too, late at night,
When stars above shine cold and bright?
Do you ask the heavens what went wrong,
Or listen to the earth's sad song?

I've felt the rain, once pure and clean,
Now tainted, with a silver sheen.
Have you tasted tears upon your tongue,
Or felt the weight of songs unsung?

Each day I walk, I feel the loss,
Of every stream, each patch of moss.
Do you mourn the things that used to be,
The chirping birds, the buzzing bees?

I speak to the wind, I talk to the trees,
Asking for wisdom, seeking peace.
Do you ever talk to the earth like me,
Or simply admire its majesty?

I've watched the seasons come and go,
With winter's chill and summer's glow.
But now it seems they're out of sync,
Do you notice, do you think?

Our earth is crying, can't you see?
It's calling out to you and me.
Do you feel the pain beneath the ground,
Or just the silence all around?

I've sat by lakes under moonlit skies,
And felt the sadness in their sighs.
Have you ever felt that heavy weight,
Of nature's sorrow, nature's fate?

I ask myself what I can do,
To make a change, to see it through.
Do you ask yourself the same,
Or think the earth is just a game?

I know the earth is more than land,
It's life, it's breath, it's something grand.
Do you see the world this way,
Or just a place where you stay?

I've seen the fires rage and burn,
Leaving behind a world upturned.
Do you feel the heat, the ash, the smoke,
Or just the sting in every choke?

We are the earth, and it is us,
Connected through this shared trust.
Do you feel this bond I speak of here,
Or see the world through the eyes unclear?

I ask you now to take a stand,
To feel the earth, to hold its hand.
Will you listen to its silent plea,
And act with love, just like me?

The earth is calling, loud and clear,
Begging for hope, for us to steer.
Will you answer, will you try,
Or let the earth's sad voice just die?

I am Siddharth, with words I weave,
A tapestry of the truths I believe.
I ask you now, with all my might,
Will you join me in this fight?

Together we can heal the earth,
Give back to it, for all it's worth.
Will you stand with me, take this vow,
To save the earth, starting now?

Let's write a new chapter, hand in hand,
Of love, respect, and understand.
Will you help me turn the page,
Or leave the earth in a silent rage?

For every tree that stands alone,
For every seed that's ever grown,
Let's make a promise, strong and true,
To care for Earth, for me and you.

The earth is crying, hear its plea,
It calls to you, it calls to me.
Will you listen, will you care,
Or leave it gasping, in despair?

I am Siddharth, my words are few,
But in them lies a world anew.
Will you join me in this quest,
To give our Earth a chance to rest?

Chapter 27. The Enigma of Dreams

Have you ever wandered in a dream,
Floating down a quiet stream?
A place where nothing's as it seems,
Where the world breaks apart at the seams?

In my sleep, I find a place,
A world that moves at its own pace.
Colors brighter, skies so wide,
Have you seen the dreams that hide?

I close my eyes and drift away,
To a realm where shadows play.
Have you felt the gentle pull,
To places strange yet wonderful?

In dreams, I've walked on distant shores,
Heard the echo of ancient wars.
Have you stood beneath the stars,
And wondered if dreams are ours?

I've touched the clouds and kissed the moon,
Danced with echoes in a silent tune.
What do you see when you close your eyes,
In a world where gravity defies?

I often wonder what dreams mean,
These midnight tales, these sights unseen.
Have you ever woken with a start,
Feeling your pulse, your beating heart?

I've seen myself from far above,
Soaring high like a restless dove.
Have you flown across the sky,
Felt the wind as you fly by?

In dreams, I've met the long-lost past,
Seen moments that would never last.
Do you remember those fleeting sights,
That linger long into the night?

I've walked through gardens of light and
shade,
Where whispered secrets never fade.
Have you heard the voice of dreams,
Soft and distant, like flowing streams?

Sometimes I wake and can't recall,
If what I saw was real at all.
Have you chased a shadow's trace,
Only to find an empty space?

I've stood on mountains made of mist,
Where every stone and leaf is kissed.
What do you see in the dream's haze,
Is it clear, or does it amaze?

I've heard songs sung by nameless birds,
Whose melodies were without words.
Have you ever heard a song so clear,
It echoes on, though none can hear?

I wonder, are dreams just random scenes,
Or do they tell us what life means?
Have you found wisdom in the night,
Or just the fading morning light?

I've felt the touch of hands unseen,
In places where I've never been.
Do you feel the grasp of dreams,
As real as water in running streams?

I've faced fears that I could not flee,
But in dreams, I always found the key.
Have you faced the monsters in your mind,
And woken to a world more kind?

I've found friends in these midnight tales,
Some who spoke, and some who were veiled.
Do you meet people in your sleep,
Who whisper secrets soft and deep?

In dreams, I've lived a thousand lives,
Seen countless worlds and countless skies.
Have you ever felt this too,
A world that's vast, yet strangely true?

I've seen the world in black and white,
And also bathed in colors bright.
What do you see in your dreams' hue,
Are they vivid, or just a faint view?

I've wandered through forests dark and deep,
Where hidden creatures softly creep.
Have you walked in shadows long,
Or found comfort in a dream's song?

I often dream of endless seas,
Rolling waves and gentle breeze.
Do you sail these oceans too,
Or stand upon the shore, just you?

I've faced the storm and found my way,
Through the darkest night to the light of day.
Have you ever been lost in dreams,
Only to find things are not what they seem?

In dreams, I've seen the world undone,
The end of time and the birth of the sun.
Do you see the end of things,
Or just the start of what life brings?

I've climbed the tallest trees, so high,
Touching the stars in a moonlit sky.
Have you ever reached for stars,
Found them close, yet still so far?

Sometimes I dream of peace so pure,
A place where everything's secure.
Have you found this sacred place,
In the silence of a dream's embrace?

I've seen cities rise from dust,
Built on dreams and powered by trust.
Do you build in dreams, like me,
Crafting worlds from what you see?

I've fallen deep into the night,
Through endless voids, without fright.
Have you felt this falling too,
Into a dream that's strange and new?

In dreams, I am both king and slave,
A hero brave, a coward who caves.
Who are you when you dream,
Do you reign, or do you scream?

I wake sometimes, tears on my face,
Lost between dream and waking space.
Have you woken with a start,
Feeling dreams tug at your heart?

I am Siddharth, a dreamer bold,
Who's wandered dreams both hot and cold.
Do you dream, as I do here,
In worlds that shift, yet feel so near?

Let's walk together through this night,
Explore these dreams until the light.
Will you share your dreams with me,
As we turn these pages of mystery?

Chapter 28. The Shadows of Lost Friendship

Once, I had a friend so dear,
We laughed and danced without fear.
Do you remember those days too,
When friendships felt so pure and true?

We used to talk for hours on end,
Dreaming big, playing pretend.
Have you felt that connection fade,
Leaving behind a shadowed shade?

Time moved on, as time will do,
Life took turns that we never knew.
Have you ever lost your way,
With a friend who chose a different day?

We promised we'd stay close, you see,
But promises aren't always free.
Did you think, like me, they'd last,
Or vanish quickly in the past?

I wonder where you are today,
What thoughts have led you far away.
Do you find yourself alone,
Missing voices once well-known?

I've thought of calling, sending a note,
But fear stops the words in my throat.
Have you ever wanted to reach out,
Yet found yourself filled with doubt?

I've heard that people grow apart,
And distance can break a tender heart.
But why do some friendships last,
While others crumble into the past?

The laughter echoes in my mind,
The secrets shared, the moments kind.
Do you replay those memories too,
Wondering what became of you?

There were fights and silly tears,
But we always found a way, my dear.
Do you believe in second chances,
Or are we stuck in these trances?

I saw you once, just the other day,
You looked at me and turned away.
Did you feel the weight of loss,
Or was our friendship just a cross?

I remember summer nights so bright,
Talking under the starry light.
Do you ever sit and sigh,
Thinking of those days gone by?

Some say it's life that pulls us apart,
But I think it's more about the heart.
Have you found new friends to hold,
Or is your heart growing cold?

I've met new faces along the way,
But no one quite like you, I'd say.
Do you compare the friends you meet,
To those who made your heart skip a beat?

Sometimes I wonder if you're well,
If you've found your heaven or your hell.
Do you look back with regret,
Or have you moved on, with no debt?

I still keep that gift you gave,
A symbol of the bond we saved.
Do you have something of mine,
That reminds you of a sweeter time?

We walked different paths, that's true,
But in my dreams, I still see you.
Do you dream of me, my friend,
Or has your heart chosen to mend?

I know it's silly to hold on tight,
To what once was, in the dead of night.
But do you sometimes feel the pull,
Of what was once so wonderful?

I miss your laugh, your silly grin,
The way you'd always let me in.
Do you miss the way we were,
Or is your life now just a blur?

I wrote this poem to say goodbye,
To all the things that made me cry.
Will you write back someday,
Or have you truly gone away?

Sometimes I think I see your face,
In a crowded, busy place.
Do you think of me too,
In moments when you're feeling blue?

We've both changed, we're not the same,
But I still whisper your name.
Do you remember who we were,
Before life's storm began to stir?

I know that things can never be,
The way they were for you and me.
But do you hold a hope, so slight,
That we might find a way, one night?

We all lose friends along the way,
It's a price we have to pay.
Have you counted those you've lost,
And wondered if it's worth the cost?

I'm Siddharth, a friend you knew,
A name you whispered, a bond we grew.
Do you remember me as I remember you,
A shadow of what once was true?

So here I sit, pen in hand,
Writing words you'll never understand.
Do you think of me at all,
Or have you forgotten every fall?

I'll leave these questions here for you,
In case you're wondering what to do.
Will you answer, or just sigh,
As our friendship fades into the sky?

Chapter 29. The Uncharted Depths of the Soul

I've wandered through the shadows of my
soul,
Dug deep to find what makes me whole.
Have you ever asked yourself, "Who am I?"
What hides beneath the surface, beyond the
sky?

I've seen reflections in a thousand eyes,
Each one showing different skies.
What do you see when you gaze within?
Is it peace, or is it sin?

Sometimes, I walk alone at night,
Lost in thoughts that take flight.
Do you feel the weight of the unknown,
Wondering what seeds you've sown?

In silence, I've heard my spirit's song,
A whisper of where I truly belong.
Have you listened to that quiet call,
Felt the rise and felt the fall?

There are moments when the mind just fades,
Lost in a maze of shifting shades.
Do you seek the truth as I do,
Or do you let the world define you?

I've chased the meaning of my name,
Through joy and sorrow, through loss and
gain.
What do you think gives life its worth?
Is it love, is it birth?

I've felt the sting of bitter tears,
Fought through doubts and countless fears.
Have you wrestled with your own despair,
Found comfort in a silent prayer?

In every heartbeat, there's a quest,
A search for peace, for endless rest.
Do you believe we're more than clay,
Crafted by hands in some grand play?

I've seen the light within my chest,
A beacon that guides, that never rests.
Do you trust that inner glow,
Or do you fear what you don't know?

I've touched the edges of my dreams,
Swam in life's relentless streams.
Do you wonder where the current leads,
To distant shores or tangled weeds?

In every dawn, there's a chance,
To learn, to grow, to find romance.
Do you see each day as new,
A canvas fresh, with skies of blue?

I've walked through forests dense and dark,
Found my way by a tiny spark.
Have you ever lost your way,
Only to find yourself in the fray?

I've felt the earth beneath my feet,
Every step, a rhythmic beat.
Do you dance to your own tune,
Or march beneath a distant moon?

I've whispered secrets to the stars,
Asked them to heal my hidden scars.
Do you share your deepest fears,
Or hide them behind layers of years?

I've climbed the mountains of my mind,
Seeking solace I hope to find.
Do you climb your own peaks high,
Chasing dreams that seem to fly?

I've watched the rivers as they flow,
Carrying stories we'll never know.
Do you let your tales unfold,
Or keep them hidden, stories untold?

In every breath, there's a story spun,
A tale of moons and rising suns.
Do you breathe with purpose clear,
Or let the winds of fate steer?

I've heard the silence loud and clear,
A sound that speaks of joy and fear.
Do you listen to your heart's own beat,
Find rhythm in each pulse and feat?

I've walked through life's vast parade,
In search of light, in search of shade.
Do you see the colors bright,
Or is your world just black and white?

I've felt the echoes of my past,
A shadow deep, long, and vast.
Do you carry your history near,
Or let it fade without a tear?

I've known the warmth of friendship's glow,
Felt the cold when it's let go.
Have you cherished those you've met,
Or lost them in the tides of regret?

I've sought answers in the skies,
Found truths in every sunrise.
Do you ask the stars above,
What is life, what is love?

I've learned that life's a fleeting dance,
A mix of fate and circumstance.
Do you think we shape our fate,
Or is it written, far too late?

I've felt the pull of the unknown,
A place where seeds of doubt are sown.
Do you leap or stand in place,
Afraid to join the endless race?

I've touched the edges of the night,
Found peace in darkness, found in light.
Do you find comfort in the dark,
Or fear it like a lurking shark?

I've asked the ocean for a sign,
To tell me where to draw the line.
Do you question what is real,
Or take life at face value, no appeal?

I've watched the shadows as they dance,
In the firelight's fickle trance.
Do you find yourself entranced,
Lost in thought, in circumstance?

I've held my soul within my hands,
Like shifting grains of desert sands.
Do you hold onto your dreams tight,
Or let them drift into the night?

I've known the power of a name,
How it can build, how it can shame.
Do you know the weight of yours,
The meaning that it underscores?

I've whispered secrets to the wind,
Confessed the places I have sinned.
Do you share your heart's true tale,
Or keep it locked, beyond the veil?

I've seen the end, I've seen the start,
Both hold space within my heart.
Do you believe in circles round,
Or think life's a line, straight, profound?

So here I stand, an open book,
Pages turning with each look.
I'm Siddharth, a poet true,
And this is my soul's view.

Chapter 30. The Silent Dance of Solitude

In the quiet corners of my mind,
I find a space, uniquely mine.
Have you ever walked this silent road?
Where thoughts are whispers, not a heavy
load?

I often sit by the window's light,
And watch the stars as they ignite.
Do you too find solace in the night,
In shadows that give way to sight?

I've felt the cold touch of loneliness' breeze,
A chill that brings me to my knees.
But in this space, I also find,
A rhythm, a beat, a dance in time.

Do you ever feel the world's weight lift,
When you surrender to this gift?
The silence speaks in its own way,
What does it tell you, night or day?

I've danced alone under the moon's pale gaze,
Lost in the moment, lost in the haze.
Have you ever felt that soft embrace,
Of solitude's warm, tender grace?

I've seen reflections in the mirror's frame,
Each one whispering my name.
Do you see yourself in every glance,
Or lose your soul in life's fast dance?

In solitude, I hear my heart's true beat,
A melody simple, pure and sweet.
Do you listen when the world grows still,
And feel your spirit start to fill?

I've wandered through fields of thought,
In solitude, these lessons taught.
What have you learned when you're alone,
In the moments when all is unknown?

There's a beauty in being by oneself,
Like an unread book on a high-up shelf.
Have you found stories untold,
In the silence that wraps you in its fold?

I've known the nights when no one calls,
Just me and my shadow on the walls.
Do you fear those empty halls,
Or find comfort in their vast, blank sprawl?

Sometimes, I've spoken to the stars above,
Asked them questions about life and love.
Do you talk to the sky at night,
Seeking answers in the dim, soft light?

I've felt the echo of my voice,
In solitude, I find my choice.
Have you heard your own words loud,
When alone, away from the crowd?

In the dance of solitude, I've found a friend,
One who stays till the very end.
Do you embrace the quiet, too,
Or chase the noise, the crowded view?

There's a power in being still,
A magic that can bend the will.
Have you harnessed this potent force,
Or let distractions change your course?

I've watched the sun rise all alone,
Its colors like secrets being shown.
Have you ever seen the dawn alone,
And felt the world's soft, gentle tone?

In moments when I'm on my own,
I realize I'm never truly alone.
Do you feel a presence near,
In the silence, do you hear?

The world may spin, loud and fast,
But solitude lets the quiet last.
Have you found that place of peace,
Where thoughts and worries cease?

I've found a love for my own space,
Where I can move at my own pace.
Do you cherish those quiet times,
When life's a poem, soft in rhymes?

I've seen the beauty in the pause,
When life takes breath, without a cause.
Do you find those moments rare,
Or do they come with a silent stare?

Sometimes, in the quiet's sway,
I lose myself, then find my way.
Have you danced in the dark, unseen,
Between the shadows, in the in-between?

There's a melody in the hush,
A song that calms the world's rush.
Have you heard that gentle tune,
Beneath the stars, beneath the moon?

I've traced my thoughts like rivers run,
Found new paths beneath the sun.
Do you explore your inner streams,
Or just float along life's seams?

In solitude, I've built my dreams,
Crafted them in moonlight beams.
What have you created in your time,
When silence is your partner in crime?

I've seen my soul in full display,
In the quiet of the break of day.
Do you look deep within your heart,
When the world's chaos falls apart?

I've found strength in the solo dance,
A freedom found in circumstance.
Do you step alone with grace,
Or hide from your own face?

Solitude, my old, true friend,
With you, I've seen beginnings, seen ends.
Do you hold your solitude tight,
Or push it away with all your might?

In the dance of silence, I've found my voice,
A quiet song that leaves no choice.
Do you hear your own refrain,
When you're alone, and it starts to rain?

I've felt the world in a single breath,
Touched the line between life and death.
Have you felt that same thin line,
In moments when stars align?

I've known the calm of a quiet mind,
A gentle peace that's hard to find.
Do you seek this quiet grace,
Or run from your own space?

In solitude's soft, sweet embrace,
I've found a true and sacred place.
Have you felt its calming hand,
As it guides you through life's land?

So here I stand, in the quiet dance,
Finding beauty in every chance.
I'm Siddharth, in solitude's glow,
And now you've walked my path, you know.

Chapter 31. Whispers of the Ancestors

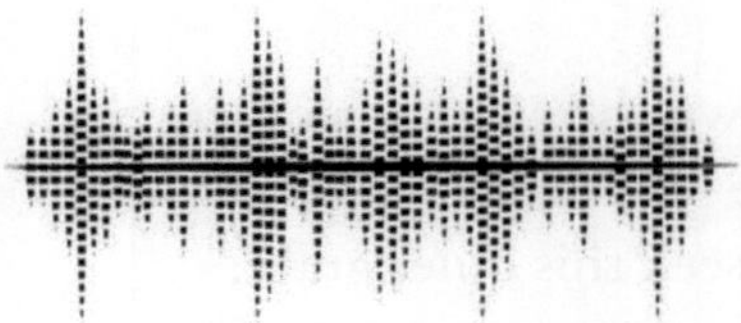

In the echoes of the old and wise,
I find a truth that never dies.
Have you ever paused to hear,
The voices from a distant year?

Stories whispered through the leaves,
Carried softly on the breeze.
Do you listen when they call,
Or let their wisdom slip and fall?

I've walked in fields where my fathers trod,
And felt the pulse of ancient gods.
Do you ever feel their might,
In the stillness of the night?

The tales of old, they speak to me,
Of battles fought and lands set free.
What stories do you hold dear,
Told by those no longer here?

My grandmother spoke of stars above,
As symbols of undying love.
Do you find guidance in the skies,
Or seek your answers in others' eyes?

Each wrinkle on my grandfather's face,
A line drawn by time's embrace.
Do you see the maps in skin,
The stories etched deep within?

I've heard the songs of pain and joy,
Sung by those long since destroyed.
What melodies do you know well,
Passed down like a treasured shell?

In kitchens warm with hearth and flame,
I learned the power of a name.
Do you taste the past in each meal,
A history you can touch and feel?

My mother spoke of rivers wide,
Where ancient spirits used to hide.
Do you wander through your dreams,
To places where the silence screams?

I've traced the steps of those before,
On paths they walked forevermore.
Do you follow where they lead,
Or forge new paths in word and deed?

The wisdom of the years gone by,
Lives in the earth, the sea, the sky.
Do you see it in a child's smile,
Or in the mountains, strong and wild?

I've sat in circles, hand in hand,
With those who knew this ancient land.
Do you partake in these sacred rites,
Or stay hidden in the night?

From every stone and blade of grass,
I hear the whispers as they pass.
Do you feel their gentle touch,
Or think the past has taught too much?

I've read the lines in ancient books,
Found wisdom in the strangest nooks.
Do you seek the old and wise,
Or close your mind to their disguise?

In the quiet of a forest deep,
I've felt the pull of time's great sweep.
Do you hear the forest speak,
Or leave its secrets for the meek?

The cries of those who came before,
Still echo on the ocean's shore.
Do you listen to their song,
Or think their time is dead and gone?

I've seen the ghosts of warriors brave,
Dance upon the grassy grave.
Do you honor them in thought and deed,
Or let their memory recede?

From lullabies to battle cries,
Their stories dance before my eyes.
Do you find the strength in lore,
Or search for truth forevermore?

The stars above, they tell me tales,
Of ships that sailed with mighty sails.
Do you dream of distant shores,
Or keep your feet on known floors?

In every tear my ancestors shed,
I find the words that go unsaid.
Do you feel their silent plea,
Or let the past simply be?

My father's words, though soft and few,
Held truths I find forever true.
Do you hear your elders' say,
Or brush their wisdom all away?

The earth itself, it hums a song,
Of life that's lived for oh so long.
Do you sense its steady beat,
Or miss the rhythm beneath your feet?

I've touched the stones of ancient walls,
Felt the chill of ghostly calls.
Do you walk in history's shoes,
Or choose your path without a clue?

I've seen my past in every tree,
Roots that stretch so far, so free.
Do you feel connected too,
To the ancient roots that carry you?

Through fire, water, earth, and air,
The voices linger everywhere.
Do you listen to their guide,
Or hide from what they have inside?

In every drop of rain that falls,
I hear the ancestors' calls.
Do you hear them in the rain,
Or see it as a mere refrain?

Their wisdom's like a river wide,
Flowing strong against the tide.
Do you swim against its flow,
Or let it take you where it goes?

From cradle to the grave, they speak,
In whispers soft and voices meek.
Do you heed their quiet word,
Or think them just an unseen herd?

I stand with those who've come and gone,
Their voices strong within my song.
I'm Siddharth, and now you see,
The past lives on, in you and me.

Chapter 32. The Hidden Language of Art

In the silent brushstrokes of a painted scene,
I find a world unseen, a place serene.
Have you ever felt the pull of a color's call,
Or seen your own story in a canvas on the
wall?

Art speaks in whispers, soft and true,
In hues of red and vibrant blue.
Do you find your voice in a painted sky,
Or in a sculpture's shape, do you ask why?

I've walked through galleries, hushed and still,
Where every frame could break or build.
Have you felt that quiet thrill,
When the art you see matches your will?

A dance, a song, a spoken word,
In every form, a message heard.
What stories do you keep within,
Hidden beneath your surface skin?

My mother's hands, they shaped the clay,
With every twist, she'd knead and play.
Do you mold your world like that too,
Creating forms from feelings true?

I've seen graffiti on old stone walls,
Bold lines that speak of freedom calls.
Do you read the words left there,
Or do you simply pass by, unaware?

In music's notes and verses long,
I hear the echoes of life's song.
Do you listen to those silent sounds,
The spaces where no noise is found?

A sculptor's chisel, sharp and fine,
Reveals the heart within the line.
Have you ever carved your pain,
Into something whole again?

The poets write in verse and prose,
Of love and loss, of highs and lows.
Do you find yourself in their rhyme,
Lost in thoughts of another time?

I've danced in shadows, light, and shade,
Each step a story, each move displayed.
Do you dance when no one's there,
Feeling free without a care?

A photograph, it stops the clock,
Capturing moments, feelings, shock.
Do you see your life in frames,
Or do you see it in the flames?

In every note a painter plays,
On a canvas that fades or stays.
Do you paint your dreams each night,
In colors bold or soft and light?

A theater stage, so grand and vast,
Where every role can change so fast.
Have you acted out your fears,
Or faced the crowd through tears?

I've written words upon a page,
A diary of thoughts, a silent rage.
Do you find solace in the pen,
Or does it bring you back again?

Art is the breath of silent screams,
A canvas filled with all our dreams.
Have you breathed this air so pure,
Or is your world a little blur?

A singer's voice, a soft caress,
Can lift the heart or cause distress.
Do you sing when all alone,
Finding comfort in the tone?

I've seen the world through many eyes,
In portraits painted with the skies.
Do you see yourself in me,
Or do you seek what you can't see?

Art speaks in every shape and form,
A storm within, a calm so warm.
Do you feel the thunder's clap,
Or the gentle lull of a map?

In every building, high or low,
An architect's dreams begin to grow.
Have you built your dreams so tall,
Or do they crumble as you fall?

I've crafted poems late at night,
Words that danced in dim twilight.
Do you write to find your way,
Or do your thoughts lead you astray?

A dancer spins, her story told,
In moves so fluid, so bold.
Do you see the story there,
In every leap and graceful air?

The hidden language of the heart,
Speaks through every form of art.
Do you listen to its voice,
Or do you think it's just a choice?

I've seen myself in pieces made,
In every line and every shade.
Do you see your truth in mine,
Or do you think it's just a sign?

Each piece of art, a hidden plea,
To be heard, to be set free.
Do you feel that same desire,
Or does your passion never tire?

Art is a mirror to the soul,
Reflecting parts that make us whole.
Do you see your face in clay,
Or does it melt and fade away?

In the silence of a gallery,
I find my peace, my clarity.
Do you seek that silent space,
Or do you find it a lonely place?

I am Siddharth, a poet's voice,
In art and words, I find my choice.
Do you hear me, do you see,
The hidden messages inside of me?

Through every brushstroke, every line,
I speak in riddles, I speak in time.
Do you decode the art I show,
Or let the mystery gently flow?

Art is a dance, a silent song,
Where every heartbeat belongs.
Do you join in with the beat,
Or do you leave it at your feet?

In every artwork, I am there,
A whispering breath, a silent prayer.
Do you feel me, in this part,
The hidden language of my heart?

Chapter 33. Echoes of Forgotten Promises

In the silence of the night, I hear a distant
call,
Echoes of promises, once made, now
forgotten by all.
Do you remember the words you said,
Or have they faded, like shadows overhead?

Promises are fragile, like whispers in the
wind,
Carried away, forgotten, but never truly
pinned.
Have you made a vow you couldn't keep,
One that now haunts you, in the silence deep?

I've walked paths where promises lie,
Scattered like leaves beneath the sky.
Do you see them, too, in your own way,
Or do they blend into the gray?

Each word we speak, each vow we make,
Leaves a mark, a ripple on the lake.
Do you feel those ripples, wide and far,
Or do they fade like a distant star?

I remember promises from long ago,
Some broken, some kept, some just for show.
Have you ever made a promise in vain,
One that now brings you only pain?

Promises forgotten, yet they linger still,
In the corners of our mind, against our will.
Do you try to forget, to leave them behind,
Or do they return, a weight on your mind?

I've seen the world through eyes of doubt,
Where promises crumble and fade out.
Do you trust the words that people say,
Or do you fear they'll fade away?

Every promise is a seed we sow,
Some grow strong, while others never show.
Do you water the seeds you've planted there,
Or do you leave them to wither, without a
care?

In the echoes of forgotten vows,
I find the truth, the here, the now.
Do you hear those echoes, too,
Reminding you of what you once knew?

I've held onto promises, tight and dear,
Even when they filled my heart with fear.
Have you held on too long,
To words that now feel wrong?

Promises made in haste,
Are often the ones we waste.
Do you take your time,
Or do you rush the rhyme?

I've learned that promises can break,
But from the shards, we can remake.
Do you pick up the pieces,
Or do you let them fall to pieces?

In every promise, there's a choice,
A decision to find your voice.
Do you speak the truth, loud and clear,
Or do you hide behind the fear?

I am Siddharth, in every rhyme,
Echoes of promises, through space and time.
Do you feel the weight of your words,
Or do they fly like fleeting birds?

In the quiet moments, I reflect,
On the promises I didn't expect.
Do you look back, to the past,
Or do you try to move on fast?

Each broken promise, a lesson learned,
A fire in the heart that once burned.
Do you learn from the pain,
Or do you let it leave a stain?

Promises forgotten, yet they find a way,
To return to us, day by day.
Do you hear their call,
Or do you build another wall?

In the echoes of the past, I see,
A reflection of what could be.
Do you see your future there,
In the promises you dare?

Every promise holds a thread,
That ties us to the things we've said.
Do you keep that thread intact,
Or do you let it fray, lose track?

I've written these words to understand,
The promises we make, the ones we hand.
Do you write your own, too,
Or do you leave them in the blue?

In the end, promises are like stars,
Shining bright, despite the scars.
Do you reach for them, high and far,
Or do you stay where you are?

Siddharth, my name, in every line,
Echoes of promises, yours and mine.
Do you hear the echo, clear and true,
As I pass this promise on to you?

Chapter 34. The Untold Stories of Strangers

In the hustle and bustle of a crowded street,
I gaze at faces, where strangers meet.
Each one a story, hidden from view,
Yet rich with dreams, both old and new.

Have you ever paused to see their eyes,
And wondered what secrets beneath them lie?
Each glance a mystery, a tale untold,
Of lives lived quietly, or boldly bold.

I'm Siddharth, in a sea of passing faces,
Seeking the truth in their silent places.
Do you wonder who they might be,
Behind the masks of their daily spree?

On the subway, a woman lost in thought,
Perhaps of battles that she once fought.
Do you see her sorrow, her hidden strife,
Or do you pass by, uncaring of her life?

In the park, a child with a vacant stare,
What dreams does he chase, in the cool
evening air?
Do you see his wonder, his innocent play,
Or does his world slip silently away?

A man in the café, with a distant gaze,
Is he reminiscing of old, happier days?
Do you sense his yearning, his silent plea,
Or do you merely sip your coffee, free?

I pass by these lives, each one so vast,
Wondering how long their stories will last.
Do you ponder their paths, the roads they've
tread,
Or do you walk on, with your own thoughts
instead?

On the street corner, a beggar's plea,
Perhaps a tale of love, lost and free.
Do you see his hardship, the life he's known,
Or do you avert your eyes, feeling alone?

A woman with a burden, carrying her child,
Her dreams perhaps shattered, her spirit
defiled.
Do you glimpse her struggles, her silent cries,
Or do you walk past, under indifferent skies?

Each face tells a story, rich and profound,
Of joy and sorrow, of life all around.
Do you listen to these tales, whispered in a
glance,
Or do you hurry by, missing the chance?

In every stranger, there's a depth unknown,
A world of experiences, a seed that's sown.
Do you reach out, to understand and see,
Or do you leave them in their mystery?

I've found that every soul has its own tale,
Of triumph and struggle, of wind and sail.
Do you see these stories as you walk your
path,
Or do you focus solely on your own
aftermath?

Strangers pass by, like leaves in the wind,
Their stories untold, their lives pinned.
Do you stop to hear their silent cries,
Or do you let their stories slip by?

I've learned that behind each passing face,
Lies a world of dreams, of hope and grace.
Do you take a moment to connect and share,
Or do you walk on, unaware?

In the quiet moments of our lives,
We find the stories where the truth thrives.
Do you listen closely to the tales around,
Or do you remain in your own world,
unbound?

I am Siddharth, and in these lines, I strive,
To uncover the stories that keep us alive.
Do you see the beauty in every stranger's eye,
Or do you let their stories simply pass by?

In the end, each life is a book, a page,
Filled with tales of joy, sorrow, and rage.
Do you turn those pages, with curiosity keen,
Or do you walk past, never truly seen?

The untold stories of strangers, I now see,
Are reflections of humanity, and of me.
Do you recognize the shared thread of our
lives,
Or do you simply let the moment pass by?

Chapter 35. The Mystery of Time's Passage

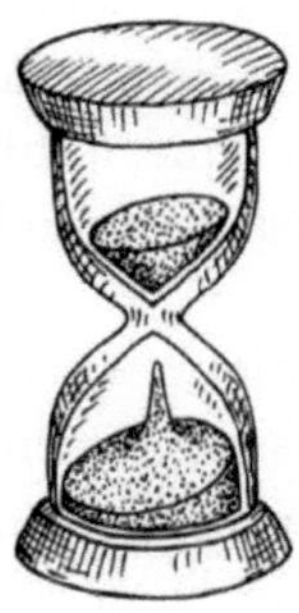

Time, an enigmatic, unyielding stream,
A force that shapes our every dream.
In its embrace, we dance and sway,
As moments drift like clouds away.

Have you ever felt its fleeting touch,
A whisper soft, yet means so much?
I, Siddharth, trace its silent course,
As time unravels, with gentle force.

I recall my youth, a vivid hue,
Now faded to memories, a distant view.
Do you see your past, like shadows cast,
In the corridors of your life, so vast?

Each tick of the clock, a moment's song,
Echoes of days that felt so long.
How does time mark your life's page,
As you move through each new stage?

The years unfold like petals in bloom,
From childhood's light to adulthood's gloom.
Do you find the same, a shift so grand,
As time's sands slip through your hand?

In the quiet of night, when stars ignite,
I ponder the passage, its endless flight.
What dreams do you chase, in time's vast sea,
As the hours drift by, so endlessly?

The footprints we leave in the sands of time,
Are etched with moments, so sublime.
Do you cherish the paths you have trod,
Or question the journey, and what you've
sought?

As I watch the seasons shift and change,
I see life's patterns, vast and strange.
How do you embrace the cycles that flow,
From summer's warmth to winter's snow?

Time teaches us with a gentle hand,
To understand life's shifting sand.
Do you feel its lessons, quiet and wise,
In the passing moments, beneath the skies?

The faces I see, in time's grand parade,
Are woven in stories, each serenely laid.
What tales do you tell of the time you've
known,
As the years pass by, and seeds are sown?

In the rush of days and the calm of night,
Time dances on, in endless flight.
How do you mark its passage, its course,
In the ebb and flow, the gentle force?

I see my reflection in time's deep well,
A witness to moments, where stories dwell.
Do you find your essence in the time you
spend,
In the moments lived, and the paths you
mend?

Each second a drop in a river so wide,
Carrying us forward, with each tide.
How do you navigate its ceaseless stream,
In the vast expanse of your life's dream?

Time, a silent witness to all we do,
A constant thread, weaving through.
Do you embrace its passage, its silent grace,
As you journey through life's endless space?

The moments we cherish, the memories we
make,
Are the treasures we hold, for time's own
sake.
Do you find joy in the fleeting now,
In the ever-moving flow, do you take a bow?

As the days turn into years, and the years into
lore,
Time marches on, forevermore.
How do you find meaning in its endless quest,
In the rhythm of life, in its gentle jest?

I, Siddharth, reflect on the mystery so grand,
Of time's passage, and the footprints we leave
in the sand.
Do you ponder its secrets, its endless song,
In the dance of moments, where we all
belong?

In the end, as time continues to flow,
We grasp at moments, both high and low.
Do you savor its gifts, its fleeting grace,
In the ever-changing, timeless space?

Chapter 36. The Silent Symphony of Night

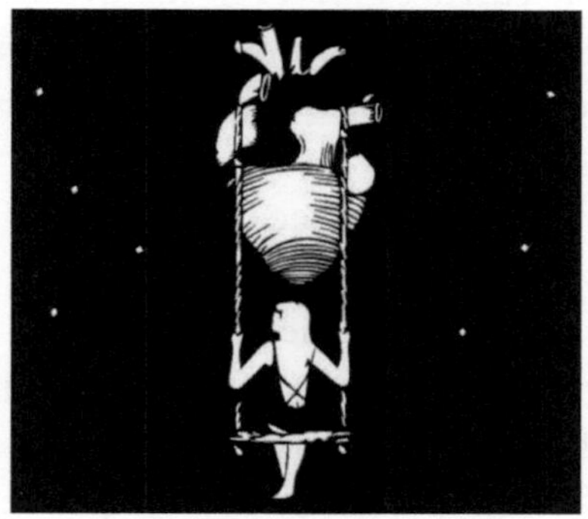

In the quiet of the night, where shadows play,
I find a symphony in the dark's soft sway.
Stars whisper secrets in the velvety sky,
And the moon hums softly as hours slip by.

Have you felt the calm when day turns to
night?
A tranquil hush where silence takes flight?
I, Siddharth, marvel at the stillness around,
In the night's embrace, where peace is found.

I walk through the dark, with steps so light,
In a world that's softened by the cloak of
night.

Do you see the beauty in the quiet scene,
Where dreams are born and the night's
serene?

The gentle rustle of leaves in the breeze,
And the distant call of night-time's pleas.
How does the night soothe your restless
mind,
In the silence, what solace do you find?

The world is hushed, the city sleeps,
While the moonlight in its stillness peeps.
Do you find comfort in the night's soft fold,
Where stories of wonder and magic are told?

The stars above, a glittering dance,
In the velvet sky, they seem to enhance.
Do you gaze at the constellations high,
And ponder the mysteries of the night sky?

In the depths of night, where shadows rest,
I seek the calm that feels the best.
What thoughts drift through your mind so
clear,
When the world is quiet and the night draws
near?

The night is a canvas, painted in deep hues,
A tapestry of tranquility, where we muse.

How do you embrace the silence so deep,
In the stillness where secrets gently seep?

In the quiet moments, where time seems to
pause,
I find peace without any cause.
Do you cherish these moments of calm so
rare,
When the world is asleep and the night's laid
bare?

The whispers of night, soft and sweet,
Wrap around me like a blanket of heat.
What dreams do you weave in the night's
gentle hold,
In the silence where your stories unfold?

The night's symphony, a melody so pure,
A gentle reminder of beauty's allure.
How does the night inspire your soul's flight,
In the harmony of stars and the moon's light?

I, Siddharth, find solace in the night's
embrace,
A refuge of quiet, a sacred space.
Do you seek the same in the night's silent
grace,
In the moments of stillness, do you find your
place?

In the depth of night, where shadows play,
I uncover a peace that guides my way.
What does the night reveal to you, so clear,
In its silent symphony, do you hold it near?

As the world slumbers and the moonlight
gleams,
I drift through a realm of ethereal dreams.
Do you listen to the night's whispered tune,
And find in its stillness a calming boon?

In the silent symphony, where the night sings,
I ponder the beauty that darkness brings.
How do you navigate through the night's
quiet grace,
In the stillness, what moments do you
embrace?

As the hours pass and the night unfolds,
I find stories in the darkness, untold.
Do you sense the magic in the night's deep
sea,
In the silent symphony, do you feel free?

In the calm of night, where shadows blend,
I discover a peace that seems to mend.
How do you cherish the night's gentle fold,
In the stillness, where your heart's stories are
told?

In the embrace of night, where whispers
dwell,
I find a quiet where peace does swell.
Do you find comfort in the night's soft song,
In the silent symphony, where you belong?

In the silent hours, where darkness reigns,
I feel the night's gentle, soothing strains.
How does the night's calm touch your soul,
In its silent symphony, do you find your
whole?

Chapter 37. The Unseen Dance of Shadows

In the twilight's hush, where light begins to
fade,
I see shadows dance, in the quiet, they parade.
Their forms are fleeting, shifting in the night,
Whispering secrets in the absence of light.

Have you ever noticed how shadows creep,
In the corners of your mind, while you're
asleep?
I, Siddharth, watch as they flicker and sway,
Reflecting our fears in a mysterious display.

The shadows lengthen as the day turns to
dusk,
Embracing our worries, our doubts, and our
trust.
Do you see them move with a silent grace,
Echoing the fears that we try to erase?

In the darkened room, where shadows play,
I confront the echoes of what's kept at bay.
Do you recognize the shapes that loom so tall,
Mirroring the insecurities we hide from all?

I find in their dance a reflection so clear,
Of the fears and doubts that we hold dear.
What do you see in the shadows' silent flight,
Is it a reflection of your inner plight?

The dance of shadows reveals more than sight,
It shows our fears in the dead of night.
Do you see the patterns in their elusive grace,
Reflecting the struggles you silently face?

In the quiet, where shadows begin to blend,
I see my own fears around the bend.
What does your shadow reveal to you,
In the soft, creeping silence, what truths come
through?

The unseen dance is a mirror, so profound,
Of the insecurities that in darkness are found.
How do you confront the shadows that play,
In the corners of your mind, as night turns to
day?

The shadows whisper tales of old and new,
A silent dialogue of what's hidden from view.
Do you listen to their whispers in the dark,
And find in their dance a hidden spark?

In the shifting light, where shadows wane,
I see the reflection of joy and pain.
How do you decipher the stories they tell,
In their silent dance, where mysteries dwell?

The dance of shadows is a timeless art,
Revealing the fears that we hide in our heart.
Do you find courage in the dance so stark,
Or are you haunted by the shadows' dark
mark?

In their movement, I see the truth unfold,
Of the fears and doubts we dare not hold.
What shadows follow you in your quest,
And how do they shape your very best?

The unseen dance is both tender and severe,
A reflection of our innermost fear.

How do you face the shadows that haunt,
In the quiet moments, where doubts taunt?

As the night stretches on, the shadows persist,
A constant reminder of the fears we resist.
Do you embrace their dance as a part of your
fight,
Or do they linger as phantoms in the night?

In the gentle sway of shadows on the wall,
I see the dance of fears, both big and small.
How do you navigate through their silent
song,
In their ever-changing forms, where do you
belong?

The dance of shadows, a mysterious play,
Revealing the depths of our fears each day.
Do you find solace in their enigmatic grace,
Or do they challenge you to confront your
own space?

In the dark, where shadows dance so free,
I uncover the fears that are part of me.
What lessons do you learn from their subtle
dance,
In the quiet of night, do you find a chance?

The unseen dance of shadows is a profound
tale,
A reflection of our fears that we often veil.
How do you face the shadows with courage
and might,
In their silent dance, do you find your light?

As the night gives way to the breaking dawn,
The shadows fade, but their lessons linger on.
Do you carry their wisdom as the day begins,
In the morning's light, where your strength
wins?

In the dance of shadows, I find a guide,
To the fears and insecurities I cannot hide.
What shadows do you dance with in the
night,
And how do they shape your path to the
light?

Chapter 38. The Secret Life of Thoughts

In the quiet realms where thoughts do dwell,
I ponder the secrets I dare not tell.
Through the corridors of my mind, I roam,
In search of the places where thoughts call
home.

Have you ever wandered through your own
mind's maze,
Where hidden thoughts drift in a mysterious
haze?
I, Siddharth, find that our thoughts are a
deep sea,
A reflection of who we are, who we wish to
be.

In the silent corners where shadows play,
Our thoughts whisper truths we hide away.
What do your thoughts reveal when night
falls,
In the secret language that the darkness calls?

Each thought is a thread in the tapestry spun,
Woven with dreams, regrets, and things
undone.
Do you see the patterns in the mind's endless
scroll,
The hidden chapters that define your soul?

I feel the weight of thoughts that deeply
linger,
Like a painter's brush or a poet's finger.
What does your inner canvas reveal in the
dark,
A masterpiece of light or a silent spark?

In the realm of thought, where mysteries lie,
I confront the echoes that never die.
Do you grapple with the voices of the past,
And the lingering shadows that forever last?

Thoughts dance in silence, in shadows, they
creep,
Into the places where our dreams and fears
sleep.

What stories do your thoughts whisper at
night,
In the quiet stillness, far from the light?

I see my fears and hopes, tangled and mixed,
In the silent dance where emotions are fixed.
How do you untangle the threads of your
mind,
To find the clarity you seek, so defined?

In the depths of thought, where echoes
resound,
I search for the meaning that's often
profound.
What does your inner voice quietly say,
When the world outside fades away?

Our thoughts are a mirror reflecting what's
true,
An intricate map of both old and new.
Do you navigate the landscapes of your mind,
Seeking the wisdom that you wish to find?

As I wander through my thoughts, both deep
and vast,
I uncover the lessons from a shadowed past.
What revelations emerge from your mental
sea,
And how do they shape the person you wish
to be?

Thoughts are like rivers, flowing and grand,
Carving out paths through the shifting sand.
Do you follow their course or build your own
stream,
In the quiet moments, do you chase a dream?

In the silence, I find both peace and strife,
A reflection of my inner life.
What does your inner dialogue reveal to you,
In the hushed tones of the morning dew?

The secret life of thoughts is a profound
space,
Where the complexities of our mind interlace.
How do you confront the labyrinth within,
And find the strength to let the light in?

In the stillness of thought, I find my way,
Navigating through the dark, where shadows
play.
What truths do you uncover in your own
mind,
As you explore the landscapes of the
undefined?

Our thoughts are a journey, both near and far,
A reflection of the person we truly are.

Do you embrace the secrets your mind may

keep,
And find solace in the depths so deep?

As the pages turn in the book of our mind,
We write the stories of what we find.
What does your inner narrative say about
you,
In the quiet moments, when the world is
askew?

The secret life of thoughts is both vast and
small,
A delicate dance in the corridors of the soul.
How do you make sense of the silent streams,
And the unspoken whispers of your dreams?

In the depths of thought, where mysteries
blend,
I seek the answers that only time can send.
What questions do you ask in the silence so
still,
And how do you find the answers that fulfill?

Through the corridors of the mind, I roam
free,
Discovering the secrets that shape the real me.
What does your own journey through
thoughts reveal,
And how do you find the strength to heal?

In the quiet realms where our thoughts reside,
We uncover the truths that we often hide.
How do you navigate your mental domain,
And embrace the wisdom that lies in the
brain?

Chapter 39. Beneath the Veil of Reality

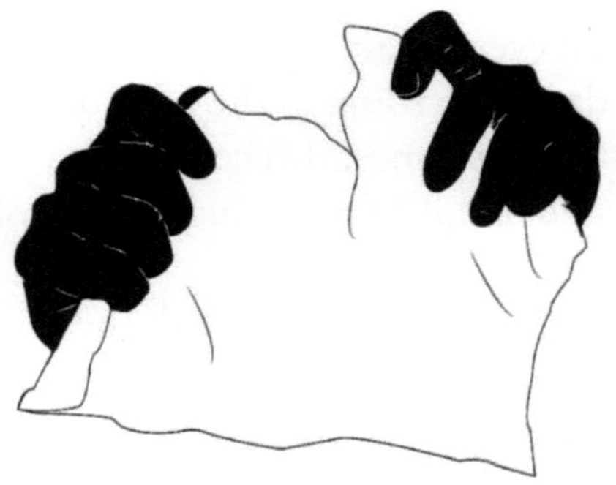

Beneath the veil of what we see,
Lies a deeper truth that sets us free.
Do we question what is real and what is mere
reflection,
Or do we live our lives in a world of
misconception?

I, Siddharth, have often pondered this
thought,
Is reality something that can be easily bought?
Do we believe only what we can touch and
see,
Or is there more to life than what appears to
be?

In the quiet moments of my day,
I ask myself if I'm on the right way.
Are my eyes deceiving me with every sight,
Is there more hidden in the dark of night?

Have you ever felt the world shift and sway,
Like a dancer twirling in the light of day?
I have felt this dance, this cosmic play,
And wondered if I too am just a piece of clay.

What if what we know is not all there is?
What if life is more than just what we miss?
I have seen shadows where there should be
none,
And felt the warmth of an invisible sun.

Do you too see beyond the surface of things,
Where reality bends and takes on wings?
In the silent hours, I hear a voice,
Asking me to make a choice.

Do we live in a world that is solid and firm,
Or is it just a fleeting term?
I've touched the edges of dreams and thought,
That perhaps our reality is naught.

Have you ever felt like you're living in a
dream?
Where nothing is quite as it may seem?

I've wandered through those twilight zones,
Where the universe hums in unknown tones.

In the quiet depths of my mind,
I search for answers I cannot find.
Do you also wonder about the truth,
And long to return to the innocence of
youth?

As I walk through this veil so thin,
I feel the truth lies within.
Do you see the layers peel away,
Revealing the night within the day?

We question the very air we breathe,
Wondering about the thoughts we weave.
Are we simply actors in a cosmic show,
Or do we have the power to know?

Reality is a mirror, reflecting back,
Our deepest fears and what we lack.
Do you find comfort in what you see,
Or is there something more you wish to be?

I have asked these questions time and again,
Trying to decipher where it all began.
Do you feel the weight of a thousand worlds,
As your mind around this mystery curls?

The truth, I believe, is beneath the veil,
Hidden in the whispers of the tale.
Do you hear the secrets in the wind,
Or feel the pulse beneath your skin?

In the silence of a thought, I find,
That reality is what we make in our mind.
Do you believe in what you feel,
Or do you think it's all surreal?

I, Siddharth, know this much is true,
Reality is shaped by what we do.
Do you agree with this simple fact,
Or does your heart hold something back?

Beneath the veil, I see the truth,
In the glimmering eyes of youth.
Do you see it too, this hidden light,
That shines in the darkest night?

We live our lives in a web so tight,
But do we see beyond the sight?
I believe there's more to see,
If we look beyond what's in front of thee.

Do you ever wonder if you're truly free,
Or if your thoughts are just debris?
I ask these questions as I roam,
Seeking the answers to bring me home.

Reality, my friend, is a shifting sea,
With waves that hide and waves that free.
Do you ride them with a steady hand,
Or do you fear to walk on sand?

In every moment, there lies a choice,
To listen to the inner voice.
Do you hear it whispering clear,
Or does it fill your heart with fear?

The veil is thin, the truth is near,
Beyond the surface, there's no fear.
Do you see the world with open eyes,
Or are you content with the disguise?

I challenge you to look within,
To seek the truth and shed the skin.
Do you accept this quest, this plea,
To discover what it means to be truly free?

In the end, it's up to us to decide,
To uncover what beneath the veil does hide.
I, Siddharth, have found my way,
Will you join me in the dance today?

Chapter 40. The Unsung Heroes of Everyday Life

In the quiet of the morning light,
When the world begins its daily fight,
I see the ones who tread unseen,
Whose humble deeds are seldom seen.

I, Siddharth, walk this path,
In search of kindness, love, and wrath.
Do you see them, too, my friend?
The ones who give without an end?

There's a lady on my street each day,
Who feeds the birds without delay.
Do you notice her gentle grace?
Or do you rush and miss her face?

In the market's crowded lane,
A boy picks up a fallen cane.
I've seen his smile, so pure and bright,
Do you, too, find such delight?

At the bus stop, just past noon,
A stranger hums a quiet tune.
He helps an elder to her seat,
Isn't such kindness bittersweet?

In this world of noise and haste,
So many moments go to waste.
Have you stopped to truly see,
The unsung heroes, just like me?

I've watched a man, with tired eyes,
Offer his coat to the cold night skies.
Do you think of him as brave?
Or a fool with nothing to save?

A mother waits with bated breath,
For her child to cross the street of death.
She prays for safety, every day,
Do you think she's just in the way?

A janitor cleans the empty halls,
When no one's there to hear his calls.
He takes pride in his simple task,
Do you see him when you pass?

These heroes wear no shiny capes,
They don't appear on glossy tapes.
I've met them in the quiet spaces,
Have you found them in hidden places?

In the corner of a bustling store,
A cashier smiles, though tired and sore.
She counts the change with a steady hand,
Have you ever made a simple stand?

I see a man who sweeps the floor,
With a heart as wide as an open door.
Do you feel the love he shows,
In every sweep, in every glow?

A gardener trims the flowers' bloom,
He hums a tune to lift the gloom.
Do you hear his silent song?
Or is your day too far along?

In a classroom, there's a teacher fair,
Who lifts the lost from deep despair.
She teaches not just facts but dreams,
Do you know what her smile means?

A nurse who holds a shaking hand,
Whispering hope like grains of sand.
Have you seen the tears she hides?
The strength she carries by our sides?

I, Siddharth, have walked these streets,
In search of heroes and humble feats.
Do you look beyond the glare,
To see the kindness everywhere?

In the shadows of a world so vast,
These heroes quietly hold us fast.
Do you feel their unseen might,
Guiding us through day and night?

A father works his second shift,
To give his child a precious gift.
He wipes his brow, he fights the fight,
Have you thought of thanking a dad tonight?

In a small café down the lane,
A barista laughs through all the pain.
She makes your coffee, strong and bold,
Have you ever said "thank you" cold?

The bus driver who knows your name,
Smiles and waves just the same.
Do you see the joy he shares,
Through the raindrops and the stares?

A neighbor helps another out,
Without a single shred of doubt.
He gives his time, he lends his ear,
Have you done the same, my dear?

There's a woman who walks each day,
With a heavy heart but a bright display.
She picks up trash along her route,
Do you know what she's all about?

In the park where children play,
A man in silence kneels to pray.
He blesses all who pass him by,
Do you ever wonder why?

In every nook, in every cranny,
Lives a soul with a heart uncanny.
I, Siddharth, have seen them all,
Have you answered their silent call?

I ask you now, my dearest friend,
To look around and comprehend.
The world is full of heroes true,
And one of them, I know, is you.

The acts of kindness, big or small,
They matter most when we give our all.
Will you join me in this quest,
To find the heroes who do their best?

Let us lift the veil of haste,
And see the beauty we've misplaced.
I, Siddharth Goswami, walk with pride,
For in your heart, these heroes abide.

Do you see them, feel them too?
In every breath, in all you do?
Let's honor those who make life bright,
The unsung heroes in the night.

For in this life, so swift and brief,
It's these small acts that bring relief.
Have you found your hero today?
Perhaps it's you, in your own way.

Chapter 41. The Untold Journey of Self-Discovery

In the quiet of the night, I wandered far,
Seeking answers in every star.
Who am I? Where do I belong?
These questions echoed, deep and long.

I, Siddharth, began this quest,
Searching for truth, for life's true zest.
Have you too felt that pull inside,
To find the place where dreams reside?

In the mirror, I saw a face,
But the soul seemed out of place.
Have you stared, eyes full of doubt,
Wondering what life's all about?

The road was winding, steep, and cold,
Yet each step felt brave and bold.
Do you fear the unknown too,
Yet march on still, seeking something new?

There were days when the sky turned gray,
When hope felt lost, just slipped away.
But in those moments, weak and frail,
Did you find strength, your inner grail?

I met strangers along the path,
Each with stories, love, and wrath.
Did you ever stop to hear,
The tales that bring both joy and fear?

In the silence, I found my voice,
In solitude, I made a choice.
To walk alone, yet not in vain,
Have you walked that road of pain?

Mountains high and valleys deep,
The journey tested what I keep.
Did you hold on to what you knew,
Or let go and start anew?

In a forest, dark and dense,
I felt lost, without defense.
Have you felt that grip of fear,
Yet pressed on, despite the tear?

Then came a light, soft and pure,
Guiding me with a promise sure.
Have you found that inner guide,
That helps you face the rising tide?

Through deserts vast and oceans wide,
I sailed on, with the stars as guide.
Did you follow your heart's desire,
Even when it set your soul on fire?

I fell, I rose, I stumbled more,
But each fall opened another door.
Have you learned from every fall,
That life's true gift is to stand tall?

I met myself in the strangest way,
In the echoes of what I didn't say.
Have you faced your own true self,
Unearthing treasures from the shelf?

In the journey, I found my name,
A truth that burns with endless flame.
Siddharth I am, with heart and might,
Do you see yourself in the light?

I questioned life, I questioned fate,
Found that love is never late.
Do you believe in love so strong,
That even the lost can belong?

In my heart, I carry scars,
Reminders of my battles and wars.
Do your wounds tell stories too,
Of battles won and dreams pursued?

I reached the peak, or so I thought,
But found the journey still not fought.
Have you ever felt that urge,
To keep on going, to truly merge?

The journey, my friend, never ends,
It twists and turns, it breaks, it bends.
Do you walk with courage, too,
Or shy away when life turns blue?

In the end, I found the key,
The truth that sets the spirit free.
Have you found what sets you right,
In the darkest hour, in the night?

Siddharth I am, in full bloom,
Carrying light in every room.
Do you carry your light, my friend,
Through the battles, till the end?

In every soul, there lies a spark,
A beacon shining through the dark.
Do you see it? Feel it burn,
Guiding you at every turn?

The journey is ours, yours and mine,
A dance of souls, a step divine.
Will you join me on this quest,
To discover what lies in our chest?

The untold journey, deep and wide,
Is where the soul and spirit glide.
Do you trust the path ahead,
Even when it's full of dread?

So I ask you, as I write,
Do you wander in the day or night?
For in each of us, there's a tale,
A journey of the strong and frail.

Siddharth Goswami, that's my name,
But you too, hold the same flame.
Will you tell your story true,
For the world, and for you?

Chapter 42. The Silence After the Storm

When the storm has passed and the winds
subside,
I stand alone, with nothing to hide.
The world is still, the chaos gone,
Have you felt that peace at dawn?

I, Siddharth, have walked this path,
Through the rage, the pain, the aftermath.
In the quiet, I found my way,
Have you too sought peace in your day?

The thunder roared, the lightning struck,
But here I am, with quiet luck.
Do you know the calm that follows fear,
When all that's left is crystal clear?

In the echoes of what once was loud,
I find my thoughts, no longer proud.
Have you felt that humble grace,
When life slows down its frantic pace?

The rain has ceased, the earth is wet,
But in this silence, I have no regret.
Do you linger in the quiet too,
When all the noise bids adieu?

I touch the earth, I breathe the air,
The storm has left, but I'm still there.
Have you felt the power in the still,
When time itself seems to stand still?

Each drop that fell, each gust that blew,
Has left a mark, both old and new.
Do you see the scars as signs,
Of battles fought and shifting lines?

In this silence, I hear my heart,
Its steady beat, a work of art.
Do you listen to your inner drum,
When the world outside is numb?

The clouds disperse, the sun peeks through,
A gentle warmth, a sky of blue.
Do you cherish these moments small,
When peace returns after all?

I, Siddharth, in this quiet found,
A piece of me, once lost, now sound.
Have you too reclaimed your soul,
In the aftermath, made yourself whole?

The storms may come, the storms may go,
But in the silence, I'll always know.
Do you find truth in the calm,
A soothing balm, a healing psalm?

I ask you now, as you read these lines,
Do you see the peace that gently shines?
For in the quiet, we find our voice,
In stillness, we make our choice.

The silence after the storm, my friend,
Is where the broken hearts mend.
Will you join me in this space,
Where life's true beauty we can embrace?

Siddharth Goswami, that's my name,
But in this silence, we're all the same.
Do you feel connected too,
In the peace that's born anew?

The storm will rage, as storms will do,
But remember, silence follows too.
Do you trust that calm will come,
After life's chaotic drum?

So here I stand, in quiet grace,
With no more need to hide or chase.
Will you find your peace with me,
In the silence after life's wild sea?

This journey of storms and quiet days,
Is a dance of life, in many ways.
Do you see the rhythm, the flow,
In the way life ebbs and glows?

So I ask, as I sign my name,
Do you feel that life's the same?
For in the calm after each storm,
We find our true and quiet form.

Chapter 43. The Hidden Pulse of Nature

I walk alone in the quiet woods,
Feeling the pulse of nature in my moods.
The rustle of leaves, the song of a bird,
Have you ever listened to the sounds
unheard?

I, Siddharth, in nature's embrace,
Find a rhythm that time can't erase.
The heartbeat of the earth, so steady and slow,
Do you ever feel it beneath your toes?

In the dance of the trees, swaying with grace,
I see a secret, an ancient trace.
Have you ever wondered what they know,
The trees that bend but never bow?

I sit by the river, watching it flow,
Its gentle current, a silent show.
Have you too sat by the water's edge,

Feeling life's calm, not its dread?

The mountains stand tall, whispering truths,
To those who listen, to the daring youths.
Have you ever climbed their rugged face,
Seeking solace in their vast space?

The stars above, twinkling bright,
Tell tales of old in the still of night.
Do you gaze at them with wonder too,
Hearing the stories that the cosmos knew?

The wind whispers secrets to those who hear,
Of life's journey, both far and near.
Have you felt its touch on your skin,
The invisible force that lies within?

I've felt the rain on my face,
Each drop a gift, a soft embrace.
Do you dance in the rain like me,
Free and wild, beneath the tree?

In the morning dew, I see the dawn,
A fresh start, a new song.
Do you see each day as a chance to be,
More than the past, wild and free?

The animals move with grace unseen,

In the hidden pulse of nature's scheme.
Have you watched them in their play,
Learning life's truths in a silent way?

I've touched the soil, warm and rich,
Felt its power, its ancient pitch.
Do you feel grounded in its might,
Connected deep, in the dead of night?

The flowers bloom, in colors bright,
A fleeting beauty, a brief delight.
Do you see the lessons they impart,
In their short lives, in nature's art?

I, Siddharth, have wandered far,
Guided by nature's quiet star.
Have you walked this path with me,
In search of life's hidden key?

The seasons change, a cycle true,
From winter's cold to summer's hue.
Do you feel the rhythm in your soul,
As nature plays its endless role?

In every rock, in every stone,
There's a story waiting to be known.
Have you ever sat and listened long,
To the earth's deep, silent song?

The ocean waves crash on the shore,

A powerful force, a mighty roar.
Have you felt its call, deep and strong,
Urging you to sing along?

The clouds drift by, soft and slow,
Casting shadows on the ground below.
Do you see the shapes they make,
Dreaming dreams that are wide awake?

I hear the call of the wild at night,
A haunting sound, a pure delight.
Have you felt that primal beat,
Echoing through your heart's retreat?

The desert sands, hot and vast,
Hold secrets of a distant past.
Have you wandered their endless miles,
Seeking truths in the ancient wiles?

In the jungle's thick, tangled maze,
I found my way through the dense haze.
Have you ever lost yourself to find,
The hidden path, the open mind?

The snow falls softly, pure and white,
A blanket of calm in the cold night.
Do you find peace in the quiet freeze,
A stillness that puts the heart at ease?

The earth is alive, in every breath,

From birth to life and even death.
Do you feel its pulse like I do,
A constant beat, a song anew?

I've sat by the fire, its warm glow,
A flickering dance, soft and slow.
Do you find warmth in its embrace,
As you sit and stare into space?

The moon rises, big and bright,
Guiding us through the darkest night.
Do you find comfort in its glow,
As it leads us where we need to go?

I, Siddharth, am part of this all,
The trees, the stars, the waterfalls.
Do you see yourself in this grand play,
A part of nature's endless day?

The hidden pulse of nature's breath,
Teaches us about life and death.
Do you listen with an open heart,
To the world that is a work of art?

In every creature, in every plant,
There's a story, a silent chant.
Have you heard the whispers too,
Of life's mysteries, old and new?

The sun sets, the day is done,

But the pulse of nature has just begun.
Will you join me in this endless dance,
Finding life's joy in every chance?

So, here I stand, in nature's grace,
A part of this world, in this sacred space.
Will you walk this path with me,
In the hidden pulse, eternally free?

Siddharth Goswami, that's my name,
But in nature's heart, we're all the same.
Do you feel the beat of this grand plan,
The hidden pulse that connects all man?

The hidden pulse of nature's song,
Reminds us where we all belong.
Will you listen, will you see,
The world's heartbeat, wild and free?

In every breath, in every beat,
Nature's pulse is pure and sweet.
Do you feel it in your soul,
The quiet rhythm that makes us whole?

And so, I leave you with this thought,
Nature's pulse is never bought.
Will you cherish it, hold it dear,
For it's the song that brings us near?

Chapter 44. The Veiled Sorrows of the Past

In the quiet corners of my mind,
I find memories, some harsh, some kind.
Have you, too, wandered these hidden lanes,
And felt the weight of past pains?

I, Siddharth, have known the night,
Where shadows danced, out of sight.
Have you ever felt their touch,
A cold grip that lingers much?

There are moments I wish to forget,
Choices made, now steeped in regret.
Do you, too, have regrets so deep,
That haunt your dreams and rob your sleep?

I recall a time, a tender day,
When words unspoken led me astray.
Have you kept your silence when you should
speak,
Only to find your heart growing weak?

The veiled sorrows, hidden away,
Whisper softly, night and day.
Do you hear them in your quiet hours,
In the stillness, amidst the flowers?

I've walked paths lined with pain,
Through storms of loss, through floods of
rain.
Have you journeyed on such roads,
Bearing burdens, heavy loads?

The past is a shadow, ever near,
A silent echo, we often fear.
Do you try to hide from its gaze,
Or face its truth through the haze?

In moments of laughter, in moments of joy,
The past sneaks in, a cunning ploy.
Have you felt its sudden sting,
Even as your heart starts to sing?

I've held onto tears, never cried,
A river of sorrow held inside.

Do you let your tears flow free,
Or hide them where none can see?

The sorrows we hide, the grief we mask,
Are they not a burden, a heavy task?
Have you ever wished to let them go,
To watch them fade, like melting snow?

I, Siddharth, have faced my fears,
Confronted ghosts from younger years.
Have you stood in front of your own past,
Demanding answers, hoping they'd last?

Each regret, each sorrow we bear,
Are stories told, if we dare.
Do you tell your stories with a sigh,
Or hold them close, afraid to try?

I've seen the eyes of those I've wronged,
Their silent forgiveness, a wordless song.
Have you sought redemption, clear and true,
For the things you wish you never knew?

The past is not just sorrow and pain;
It's lessons learned, it's wisdom gained.
Do you see it as a guide so wise,
Or a burden that never dies?

I find solace in the quiet night,
Where the moon gives a softer light.
Have you found peace in the darkest hours,
In silence, in dreams, in unseen powers?

We all carry wounds, some deep, some small,
But do they not make us human, after all?
Do you see your scars as badges worn,
Proof of battles fought, of lives reborn?

I've danced with shadows, I've danced with
light,
Embraced the day, feared the night.
Do you find strength in what's been,
In every loss, in every win?

I ask myself, day by day,
Why the past won't fade away.
Do you ask the same, with a sigh,
Watching the years slowly pass by?

The veiled sorrows, they shape our fate,
Teaching us patience, teaching us to wait.
Do you see their hidden grace,
In every tear, in every trace?

I, Siddharth, look to the sky,
Seeking answers, asking why.
Do you search for meaning in the stars,
Or let the questions drift afar?

The past, a teacher, stern and true,
Guides us toward a future new.
Do you see its lessons, bright and clear,
Or let them cloud your path with fear?

I've learned to live with what has been,
To find the strength that lies within.
Have you found that strength in you,
To face the past and start anew?

The sorrows that linger, they make us whole,
They carve their mark upon our soul.
Do you see them as friends, not foes,
Helping you to grow and know?

In the mirror, I see my face,
A reflection of time, of endless chase.
Do you see your own past there,
In every line, in every stare?

I ask myself, with a knowing smile,
Is the past just another mile?
Do you walk it like a path untold,
Discovering life as it unfolds?

The veiled sorrows, they come and go,
Like tides that ebb, like winds that blow.
Do you ride their waves, high and low,
Finding peace in their flow?

I've made my peace with what's gone by,
Letting go with a whispered sigh.
Have you too found that release,
In the quiet, in the peace?

The past is a tale we all must write,
A story that turns from dark to light.
Do you write yours with careful hand,
Or let it drift like shifting sand?

I stand now, in the present's grace,
The past a shadow I can face.
Will you stand with me, side by side,
Facing the sorrows we often hide?

In every heartbeat, in every breath,
The past lives on, beyond death.
Do you hear it, feel its beat,
In every step, in every feat?

I, Siddharth, have found my way,
Through nights of sorrow, into day.
Will you walk this path with me,
In search of life's true mystery?

The veiled sorrows of the past,
They whisper truths that forever last.
Will you listen, will you hear,
The hidden songs that draw us near?

And so, my friend, I leave you this,
A simple thought, a gentle kiss.
Will you embrace your past with grace,
And find your place in life's vast space?

Siddharth Goswami, that's my name,
But in your heart, we're all the same.
Do you see yourself in these lines,
A part of this world, intertwined?

The sorrows we hide, they are ours to keep,
But in their embrace, we find what's deep.
Will you uncover their hidden gold,
In every tale, in every fold?

The past is a friend, a guide so true,
Teaching us what we never knew.
Will you let it be your light,
Guiding you through the darkest night?

Chapter 45. The Quiet Power of Hope

In the quiet corners of my mind,
Where shadows stretch and light is blind,
I've often wandered, lost in thought,
Seeking answers that can't be bought.

Have you, dear reader, ever been,
In moments silent, so serene?
When life's storm seems too strong,
And days feel endlessly long?

I've stood upon those cliffs of doubt,
Where every whisper turns to shout.
In darkness, when no stars appear,
I found hope, a flame so clear.

It starts so small, a flickering light,
A gentle glow in endless night.
Have you ever felt its touch?
A soothing balm when life's too much?

Like rivers flowing to the sea,
Hope gently whispered back to me.
It said, "In all this vast despair,
There's a strength in simply being there."

So I learned, as we all do,
To hold on tight and see it through.
For in each trial, and every test,
Hope resides within our chest.

And you, my friend, do you feel it too?
A quiet force that pulls you through?
In moments when the world's gone dark,
Hope remains, a steady spark.

From sleepless nights to weary days,
It's hope that leads us through the maze.
It's in each breath, each step we take,
A promise that we won't break.

I remember days when tears would fall,
When I felt so small, so very small.
But hope came softly, held my hand,
And whispered, "You will understand."

Can you see it now, within your heart?
That quiet power, a humble start?
It's the whisper in the storm,
The fire that keeps us warm.

In silence, when the world retreats,
Hope gently, quietly beats.
It's in the spaces in between,
Where truth and grace are often seen.

And I, Siddharth, have come to know,
That even in the deepest woe,
Hope can grow, rise, and sing,
It's the essence of everything.

Do you find it, in the darkest hour,
This tiny, mighty, sacred power?
It's there in you, as it is in me,
A quiet strength that sets us free.

For when the world seems harsh and cold,
And you feel like you've lost your hold,
Remember, hope is always near,
A whisper soft that we can hear.

It's not in shouts or grand displays,
But in the calmness of gentle days.
It's in the rising of the sun,
In every battle lost and won.

Have you felt it in the rain?
In tears that cleanse the deepest pain?
Hope's in every drop that falls,
In every answer that life calls.

For I've seen it in the eyes of friends,
In every start and every end.
It's the strength to stand once more,
To walk beyond the open door.

And as I write, I ask of you,
To look within, to feel it too.
For hope is not a distant star,
It's here, it's now, just where you are.

So when you feel the night is long,
Remember this, in my simple song:
Hope is yours, as it is mine,
A quiet power, pure, divine.

And if you ever lose your way,
When skies are dark and clouds are gray,
Just close your eyes, take a breath,
Feel hope rise, defy death.

For in each heart, it softly blooms,
Through life's storms and empty rooms.
A testament to all we've faced,
To every fear and every haste.

Can you sense it now, in this line,
Hope so quiet, yet so fine?
It's not just words on a page,
But a lifeline, in every age.

So here I stand, Siddharth by name,
A witness to this eternal flame.
It's in our souls, this hope we keep,
A quiet power, vast and deep.

And you, dear reader, do you see?
The quiet power, that sets us free?
It's hope, simple, pure, and clear,
A gentle whisper, always near.

Chapter 46. The Invisible Bonds of Humanity

In every face, in every place,
There's an unseen bond, a shared grace.
Have you ever felt it in a crowd,
That whispering connection, speaking loud?

I've walked the paths both near and far,
From city lights to where the wild things are.
In every step, I find a thread,
Linking lives, from birth to bed.

Do you feel it, when you glance around,
The silent pulse that keeps us bound?
In laughter shared and tears we weep,
In promises that we must keep.

I've seen it in a mother's eyes,
In the way her heart just never lies.
In a father's hand, firm yet light,
Guiding his child into the night.

Isn't it strange how we all share,
This unseen web, this need to care?
Even when words are left unsaid,
There's a connection, like a thread.

Siddharth here, pondering the unseen,
These invisible ties, what do they mean?
In the smiles of strangers, passing by,
In the shared glance, the knowing sigh.

Have you felt it in a helping hand,
In a friend's support when you can't stand?
In a moment of joy, a moment of pain,
In sunlight's warmth, or in pouring rain?

I've felt it in my darkest hour,
An unseen bond, a subtle power.
When life seemed cold, devoid of light,
I found warmth in that shared sight.

Do you believe in this unseen force,
Guiding us gently, keeping us on course?
In every act of kindness shown,
In every way our love is known?

It's there, in the quiet of a prayer,
In the stories that we all share.
In every life, in every soul,
An unseen thread that makes us whole.

And what of you, have you noticed too,
These bonds that stretch, these ties that glue?
In every heartache, every cheer,
We are all connected, my dear.

I've watched the sunset, felt its glow,
Seen it touch both high and low.
No matter where its light may reach,
We're bound together, each to each.

Can you see it in a stranger's smile,
In the way it lingers for a while?
A simple act, yet profound,
A silent bond that does astound.

And I, Siddharth, have come to see,
This quiet truth, its mystery.
In every moment, large or small,
We're bound together, one and all.

In a child's laugh, in an elder's gaze,
In a friend who knows all your ways.
There's an invisible line that binds us tight,
An unseen glow, a shared light.

So tell me now, do you agree?
Do you feel this bond, so free?
In every breath, in every beat,
We find each other, we complete.

I've found it in the darkest night,
In the way stars share their light.
In the vast, unending sky,
We're linked together, you and I.

And when we stumble, when we fall,
This bond holds us through it all.
Have you felt its gentle touch,
A whisper saying, "You are enough"?

It's in the way we love and lose,
In every path we choose to choose.
An unspoken truth, always there,
A silent promise that we share.

In the laughter and in the tears,
In the courage to face our fears.
We are bound, in joy, in strife,
In every chapter of this life.

Have you ever stopped to see,
How connected we can be?
In every face, in every smile,
We find a friend, if just for a while.

And so, Siddharth, I ask of you,
To see this bond, so real, so true.
In every heart, in every hand,
Together, we all stand.

For in this world of endless space,
We're bound by love, a shared grace.
In every corner, in every land,
We're linked together, hand in hand.

So let's cherish these ties, unseen yet strong,
In every right and every wrong.
For in the end, it's clear to see,
We are all one, you and me.

Have you felt it, in your soul,
This connection that makes us whole?
It's in every breath, every sigh,
The invisible bonds that never die.

Chapter 47. Secrets of Secret Desires

In the quiet corners of our hearts,
Secrets of desires, where each story starts.
Have you ever wondered, in the still of night,
What dreams and wishes lie just out of sight?

I am Siddharth, in this journey with you,
Exploring what's hidden, both old and new.
Do you feel the stirrings, both deep and true,
Of desires that paint our world in hues?

In every glance, in every touch,
We seek connections, we yearn for much.
Have you felt the thrill of a secret glance,
Or wished for a moment, a fleeting chance?

Homosexuality, a dance of love's embrace,
In hearts where desires find their place.
Do you see love's truth in every form,
In hearts that beat both wild and warm?

I've seen love bloom in colors bright,
In same-sex unions, a shared delight.
Have you witnessed the beauty of love
unbound,
In couples who cherish, who are truly found?

And heterosexual hearts, where desires meet,
In traditional love, so tender and sweet.
Do you understand the longing's fire,
In bonds that aspire to reach ever higher?

In my own life, I've felt love's array,
From quiet moments to passionate sway.
Do you feel the pulse of your own desire,
As it fuels your dreams, lifts you higher?

Secrets of desire, both hidden and clear,
In every heartbeat, in every tear.
Have you ever wished to explore the deep,
To understand the desires you keep?

The longing in each of us, so pure,
Seeks connection, seeks to endure.
Do you see the common thread in our desires,
The way we all dance around love's fires?

I've seen love's forms, both old and new,
In hearts where passion flows through.
Do you celebrate love in all its grace,
In every form, in every embrace?

In the silence of the night, desires whisper
low,
In each of us, there's more to know.
Have you listened to your heart's secret song,
Or wondered where your desires belong?

I've found beauty in love's vast sea,
In hearts of every shape and decree.
Do you find joy in love's many forms,
In hearts that beat through calm and storms?

Love's desires are not just black or white,
But a spectrum of feelings, vibrant and
bright.
Do you see beyond the surface, the obvious
line,
To the depth of love where desires
intertwine?

In my own journey, I've learned to see,
The power of love in its diversity.
Do you honor love in every guise,
In each heartfelt glance, in each soft sigh?

Secrets of desire, they shape who we are,
They guide us through life, near and far.
Do you feel the pull of your deepest dreams,
In every whisper, in every beam?

I've walked paths where desires meet,
In moments tender, in passion sweet.
Do you embrace your own heart's call,
Or hide it away, afraid of it all?

In every touch, in every kiss,
Desires tell us what we might miss.
Have you ever felt the magic of the unknown,
In a love that's pure, in a love that's shown?

Homosexual or heterosexual, it's all the same,
In the dance of desire, in love's true name.
Do you see love's beauty in its many forms,
In every heart that breaks, in every heart that
warms?

I've felt the pulse of desire, strong and true,
In hearts that beat, both old and new.
Do you find joy in the secrets we share,
In the love that's felt, in the love that's rare?

Desires are the whispers of our soul,
Guiding us toward our deepest goal.
Do you listen to your own heart's plea,
In the secrets of desire that set you free?

In every story, in every heart,
Desires play their own part.
Have you uncovered your own hidden flame,
In the desires that have no name?

I've learned that love knows no bounds,
It lives in every whisper, every sound.
Do you celebrate love in its every hue,
In the desires that make you, you?

The secrets we keep, the desires we hide,
Are part of our journey, part of our stride.
Do you embrace your own desires true,
Or shy away from what's meant for you?

In the tapestry of love's grand design,
Desires weave their threads fine.
Do you see the beauty in each thread,
In every desire that's quietly said?

I, Siddharth, have found peace in love's
embrace,
In the secrets and desires that time cannot
erase.
Will you walk with me through this dance,
Embracing desires, taking your chance?

The secrets of desire, they shape our lives,
In every heartbeat, in every strive.

Do you honor the desires that lie within,
In every moment, in every win?

So let us cherish the desires we hold,
In every story that's yet to be told.
Will you explore your own heart's plea,
In the secrets of desires that set you free?

In every glance, in every sigh,
Desires tell us why we fly.
Do you see the truth in love's sweet call,
In every desire, in every fall?

I, Siddharth, share these thoughts with you,
In hopes that your heart finds what's true.
Will you embrace the secrets of your own
heart,
And let love and desires play their part?

Chapter 48. The Secrets Written in the Stars

In the hush of night, where dreams entwine,
I look to the heavens, where stars align.
I'm Siddharth, exploring the cosmic dance,
Wondering if the stars hold our chance.

Have you ever gazed at the starry dome,
And felt it whisper, calling you home?
In the vast expanse, where mysteries lie,
Do you see the truths that the heavens imply?

Each twinkling light, a story to tell,
Of ancient wisdom and cosmic spell.

Have you felt the magic in the night's
embrace,
In the silence of space, in its tranquil grace?

I find solace in the stellar view,
In the constellations that guide me through.
Do you see patterns in the cosmic sea,
In the paths that are drawn, in the light that's
free?

The stars above, they shimmer and gleam,
Like fragments of an eternal dream.
Have you ever felt their guiding hand,
Leading you to a far-off land?

In my own life, I've felt their light,
Guiding me through the darkest night.
Do you seek the stars' serene advice,
In moments of doubt, in moments precise?

The sky reveals a tapestry so grand,
Woven with threads from a distant land.
Do you feel connected to the starry skies,
In the way they shine, in their ancient guise?

Have you wondered about the ancient lore,
That speaks of stars and tales galore?
In the constellations that etch the night,
Do you see the messages in their light?

I've marveled at the Milky Way's sweep,
In its vast embrace, where secrets sleep.
Do you dream of exploring the cosmic stream,
Of understanding the stars' silent dream?

The secrets written in the celestial scroll,
Whisper of truths that touch the soul.
Have you ever felt their deep, silent call,
In the vast expanse, where shadows fall?

Stars may seem distant, but they're near,
In their glow, our hopes appear.
Do you feel their warmth on a cold, clear
night,
In their distant shine, in their ancient light?

I've traced the patterns in the sky's grand art,
Finding reflections of the human heart.
Do you see your own story in the cosmic
weave,
In the constellations that never leave?

In every star, a story lies,
Of dreams that soar and hopes that rise.
Have you felt the pull of their timeless grace,
In the endless night, in their silent embrace?

The night sky is a book, open wide,

With chapters of wonder that never hide.
Do you read the stars like an open scroll,
In their glowing ink, do you find your soul?

I've seen the universe in its grand expanse,
In every star's twinkle, in every glance.
Do you see the threads that weave the night,
In the patterns that dance, in the starlight?

The secrets of the stars, they gently unfold,
In tales of wonder, in stories untold.
Have you ever felt their silent guide,
In the cosmic dance, where mysteries reside?

In every shimmer, in every light,
The stars reveal their wisdom bright.
Do you find comfort in their ancient glow,
In the mysteries they share, in the truths they
show?

I, Siddharth, explore the cosmic expanse,
In the night sky's silent, mystic dance.
Will you join me in this stellar quest,
In seeking the stars and their timeless rest?

So let's embrace the secrets of the night,
In the stars' soft glow, in their quiet might.
Do you feel the call of the heavens high,
In their ancient dance, in their endless sky?

The stars above, with their silent gaze,
Guide us through our nights and days.
Do you see the beauty in their distant light,
In the secrets they hold, in their cosmic
flight?

Let us ponder the mysteries they share,
In the night sky's vast, eternal flare.
Will you find your truth in the stars so bright,
In their silent whispers, in their guiding light?

Chapter 49. The Unheard Voices of History

In the echoes of time, where shadows play,
I seek the stories that have slipped away.
I'm Siddharth, in the corridors of the past,
Where forgotten voices whisper at last.

Have you ever pondered the tales untold,
Of lives that flickered but never grew bold?
In the history we read, do you see the gaps,
Where silent voices lie in their unmarked
maps?

I wander through the annals of lost days,
Finding the paths that history sways.

Do you hear the murmur of the unheard
plight,
In the tales obscured from the broad daylight?

In the silent halls of history's keep,
Lie the stories that time did not reap.
Do you sense the weight of those unsung
names,
In the echoes of their forgotten claims?

I've unearthed tales from the dusty tome,
Of those who roamed but never found home.
Have you felt the sting of their silent cry,
In the void of history, where they silently lie?

Each whisper in the wind, a story so deep,
Of struggles and triumphs, of promises to
keep.
Do you recognize their courage and strife,
In the remnants of their overlooked life?

The pages of history often veil,
The voices of those whose stories pale.
Do you see the shadows that linger near,
In the silent gaps that history does not clear?

I've seen the footprints left in the sand,
Of those who fought but never did stand.

Have you felt their presence, strong and
grand,
In the echoes of time, in the unmarked land?

From ancient lands to modern day,
The voices lost are still here to say.
Do you hear their whispers in the rustling
leaves,
In the silent cries of those who grieve?

The past holds tales of strength and pain,
Of dreams deferred and battles lain.
Have you ever tried to lift the veil,
To listen to the voices that never prevail?

I've traced the stories through history's haze,
Finding the light in their forgotten ways.
Do you seek the truth in the obscured past,
In the voices that history could not cast?

In every silent shadow, a tale does hide,
Of lives uncelebrated, of truth denied.
Do you feel the weight of their unseen plight,
In the chronicles that are not written right?

The unheard voices speak to me,
In the silence of history's decree.
Do you hear their call in the still of the night,
In the stories that drift beyond our sight?

I've walked the paths where history sleeps,
Unearthing secrets that silence keeps.
Do you see the echoes in the shadows cast,
In the stories of the unremembered past?

The past is rich with untold grace,
Of lives that time did not embrace.
Have you ever felt the pulse of their dreams,
In the silent moments where history seems?

Each voice lost is a lesson we bear,
Of struggles and victories we must repair.
Do you find the strength in their silent fight,
In the whispers of history that come to light?

I, Siddharth, bring these voices to you,
In the hope their stories will renew.
Will you join me in this quest for truth,
In the silent cries of forgotten youth?

So let us honor the tales unsaid,
Of lives that history left in dread.
Do you hear their voices in the night,
In the silent echoes of their unspoken fight?

In every forgotten name, a spark remains,
Of courage and hope that never wanes.
Do you see the beauty in their hidden grace,
In the tales that time did not embrace?

Let us lift the veil from the shadows cast,
And give voice to the stories of the past.
Will you hear the echoes of history's plight,
In the stories of those who were never in
sight?

Chapter 50. Turning the Final Page

As I, Siddharth Goswami, stand at this stage,
I find myself turning the final page.
Have you ever wondered what lies beyond the known,
When all we have lived is a seed that's grown?

What if every ending is but a start,
A closing door that opens another part?
I have walked through chapters, each a different hue,
But what remains, I ask, when they're all through?

Do you feel the weight of the moments
passed?
The echoes of memories, both slow and fast?
I've seen joys, felt sorrows, embraced the
unknown,
Through each word written, my soul has
grown.

Isn't life a story with twists and turns,
A fire that fades and yet brightly burns?
In my journey, I've found truth in the tears,
A melody of laughter that still perseveres.

Have you faced the darkness, the shadows
deep?
The kind that whispers to you as you sleep?
I've been there too, on nights long and cold,
Yet found a spark that's warm, not old.

Do you ever ponder what tomorrow will
bring,
Or do you find peace in the song life sings?
I've chased the wind, touched the rain,
Learned that with each loss, there's something
to gain.

What does it mean to reach the end?
Is it the fall, or the chance to ascend?
For me, every ending is a doorway wide,
A chance to discover what's on the other side.

Do you fear the silence that endings hold,
Or do you find comfort as stories unfold?
I've learned to dance in the quiet of the night,
To find strength in the softest light.

Have you found yourself in the turning of a
page,
Caught between freedom and a self-made
cage?
I've been lost in those lines, bound by my
own,
Yet each chapter has led me back home.

Is it strange to find peace in a word unsaid,
To feel alive where others feel dread?
I've found that silence speaks in profound
ways,
In the pauses, the spaces between our days.

Do you trust the unknown, the paths unseen?
Or do you cling tightly to where you've been?
I've walked in shadows and basked in the sun,
Learning that both are needed for a journey
well run.

Have you ever danced to a tune without
sound,
Or felt a connection that knows no bounds?
I've heard the music that's felt, not heard,
A rhythm of life that can't be disturbed.

Isn't it strange how we fear the end,
Yet crave the new beginnings they send?
I've stood on the brink of endings, feared the
fall,
But found that the jump wasn't scary at all.

Do you see the beauty in the final bow,
In the quiet acceptance of the here and now?
I've come to cherish the moments that last,
For they shape the future, honor the past.

Do you think of endings as a full stop,
Or a comma in life's ongoing plot?
I've found them to be pauses, breaths to take,
Spaces for reflection, choices to make.

Are you ready to turn your final page,
To embrace what comes with a heart of sage?
I, Siddharth Goswami, stand ready and still,
For in every ending, I find my will.

Have you felt the fear of the unknown,
The chill of walking paths unshown?
I've felt it too, but in that fear,
I've also found what I hold dear.

Do you see life as a script to follow,
Or a blank canvas, wide and hollow?
I've painted my life with colors bright,
Embracing both the day and the night.

Will you join me as we turn this page,
Together stepping onto life's next stage?
For in the end, we are not alone,
Every story, every soul finds its home.

In this final page, we find not despair,
But the hope of a future we can share.
So let us embrace this ending, not with fear,
But with the joy of knowing, the next is near.

Do you see now, what I've tried to convey?
That every end brings a brighter day?
I, Siddharth Goswami, leave you with this
thought:
In the turning of the final page, we are never
lost.

Printed by Libri Plureos GmbH in Hamburg, Germany